Finally, a book on culture for the 21st century. I've lived and worked around the world and this book is packed full of practical insight that inspires and challenges in equal measure. In many ways it should be read by everyone; at least everyone wanting to successively navigate today's complexity and contribute to making a better and more inclusive world.

Toby Peyton-Jones OBE, former HR Director,
Siemens UK & Northern Europe

A brilliant, comprehensive overview of what it really takes to work effectively in our increasingly multi-cultural world. Thought-provoking and practical, *Bridge the Culture Gaps* challenges conventional ideas and develops new approaches for all those engaged in cross-cultural business activities.

Patrick Schmidt, former President, SIETAR Europa

With his long experience of providing training around the world for a multinational company, Robert Gibson knows best how culture affects people's success in doing business both locally and globally.

Marion Horstmann, former Corporate Vice President, Siemens

Pioneering business interculturalist Robert Gibson is better qualified than most to help readers bridge the culture gaps. His many years as in-house intercultural consultant with one of Europe's most significant global players have given him a range of intercultural experience and insight unique in their breadth and richness.

Professor Peter Franklin, Konstanz University of
Applied Sciences

Having worked in multinational corporations for 15 years managing complex interfaces and now in my third regional role, I highly appreciate the practical advice in this book. The exercises, tools and advice are ideal for use by members of diverse teams seeking to develop their global competence.

**Qing Hua Xing, former Vice President,
Head of HR Asia-Pacific, Osram.**

From my experience of being involved in M&A projects in a global corporation I know that the cultural aspects are key but often neglected. The information and practical tools which Robert Gibson provides in this book will be an invaluable help to bridge the gaps in all post-merger integration projects where 'worlds are clashing' on all levels of business organizations.

**Beate Bidjanbeg, former Director Center of Competence
M&A Integration, Siemens**

Working in a global team – often with colleagues who are working remotely from different locations – is usually exciting at the beginning before turning into nightmare when first deadlines approach and misunderstandings begin. I am delighted to see Robert Gibson approaching this delicate problem with wisdom but also practical advice that could help a multicultural team to find the right formula and perform at its best.

**Marcello Russo, Director of Global MBA,
Bologna Business School**

Robert Gibson provides the perfect overview of intercultural issues both for those starting out in the field and also for more experienced practitioners. In addition to a clear presentation of basic intercultural concepts, the book explores topical subjects such as the benefits of diversity and inclusivity for organizations and the problem of unconscious bias. Gibson's combination of academic and industrial experience makes him the ideal person to guide readers through these complex and often controversial areas.

Ian McMaster, Editor-in-Chief, Business Spotlight

Bridge the Culture Gaps

A toolkit for effective collaboration in the diverse, global workplace

Robert Gibson

NICHOLAS BREALEY
PUBLISHING

London • Boston

First published by Nicholas Brealey Publishing in 2021
An imprint of John Murray Press
A division of Hodder & Stoughton Ltd,
An Hachette UK company

2

A CIP catalogue record for this title is available from the British Library

Trade Paperback ISBN 9781529382150
eBook ISBN 9781529382174 UK / 9781529383027 US

Typeset by KnowledgeWorks Global Ltd.

Printed and bound in Great Britain by Clays Ltd, Elcograf S.p.A.

John Murray Press policy is to use papers that are natural, renewable
and recyclable products and made from wood grown in sustainable
forests. The logging and manufacturing processes are expected to
conform to the environmental regulations of the country of origin.

John Murray Press
Carmelite House
50 Victoria
Embankment
London EC4Y 0DZ

Nicholas Brealey Publishing
Hachette Book Group
Market Place, Center 53,
State Street
Boston, MA 02109, USA

www.nicholasbrealey.com

Contents

Introduction   vii

Chapter 1 Mind the Gaps: The Impact of Culture   1

Chapter 2 Globality Check: Intercultural Competence   17

Chapter 3 Return on Diversity: The Power of Difference   27

Chapter 4 Brains and Bells: Making Better Decisions   43

Chapter 5 The Intercultural Cocktail: Navigating Cultures   59

Chapter 6 Decoding the Message: Intercultural Communication 77

Chapter 7 Remotely Together: Global Virtual Collaboration   95

Chapter 8 1 + 1 = 3: Inclusive Leadership   111

Chapter 9 Oiling the Works: Influencing to Win   127

Chapter 10 The Roller Coaster: Managing Global Change   139

Chapter 11 The Barometer: Coping with International
Assignments   151

Chapter 12 Building Bridges: Strategies for Success   163

Answer Key   179
References   199
Index   207
About the Author   211
Acknowledgements   213

Introduction

Globalization is dramatically increasing the need for ways of working effectively in the diverse workplace. In response to this, the intercultural field has grown significantly over the last 30 years. Researchers are now challenging conventional ideas and developing new approaches, while neuroscience is providing fascinating insights into how the brain works. *Bridge the Culture Gaps* seeks to provide you with easy access to a selection of the most useful models and tools.

Aims

Bridge the Culture Gaps is a practical self-help guide which aims to help you optimize your performance when working in an intercultural environment. It aims not only to help you increase your awareness of differences but also to find ways of using them to positive effect.

It helps you to:

- understand the impact of culture and diversity in business

- mitigate bias to help create an inclusive workplace

- work more effectively in diverse, global teams

- leverage difference for business success.

Target group

Bridge the Culture Gaps is designed for a wide range of people who work in diverse teams and across cultures including:

- business travellers
- delegates on international assignments
- managers
- project managers
- leaders and members of diverse teams
- human resources professionals
- students and teachers of Business Administration and Intercultural Management
- intercultural trainers and consultants.

Special features

Bridge the Culture Gaps:

- covers different types of culture, including national cultures
- connects diversity and culture
- is aimed at all team members, including leaders
- is based on authentic business examples
- is interactive, with numerous exercises
- provides practical tools and tips
- is written in clear English for an international audience.

Structure

Bridge the Culture Gaps contains:

- **Key questions** at the beginning of each chapter. Take a few moments to think about them before you read on.

- **Exercises and activities** to encourage thought and self-reflection. Many of them are also suitable for use in groups. If possible, do them together with team members or other colleagues. They include:
  - *Critical incidents* – memorable situations in which cultural factors play a role. Sometimes it is difficult to isolate culture from the other factors which might determine what has happened, such as the personalities of the people involved or the particular situation that you found yourself in. The descriptions are short, so you may feel you don't have enough information. The challenge is to analyse the incident on what you do know and give provisional advice. As the details and context are up to your imagination, multiple explanations are possible.
  - *Cases* – longer descriptions of broader scenarios.

Where possible the names of countries and nationalities have been removed so that you are not influenced by stereotypes while reading the case. The original identities can be found in the answer key.

You are invited to use the **OAR** approach:
- **Observe and describe.** What happened? A neutral description of what happened, avoiding judgements and evaluation.
- **Analyse.** Why did it happen? Use your knowledge of culture to understand why something happened.
- **Recommend.** What can be done? Think about what the options might be for dealing with the situation.

- **Tools:** models or instruments which you can use in a range of situations to optimize collaboration.

- **Going further:** useful sources if you want to go deeper into the topic.

- **Answer key:** at the end of the book, you will find comments on and possible answers to the exercises, critical incidents and cases. They are designed as a guide rather than as definitive solutions.

Cultural limits

Although every effort has been made to include views and examples from as many different cultures as possible, the book is inevitably limited by the experience and perspective of the author. Hopefully, readers with different experiences and views of the world will feel stimulated to engage with the ideas presented here and adapt them for use in their own contexts.

1

Mind the Gaps

The Impact of Culture

The real voyage of discovery consists not in seeking new landscapes, but in having new eyes.

Marcel Proust

Key questions

Why are cultural differences important?

What is culture?

Exercise 1.1

Before you start to read think about your attitude to culture. The exercise prepares you for the main topics covered in this book. If possible, discuss the statements briefly with a colleague or your team.

What do you think about the following statements?

1. Globalization means that there is now a standard business culture everywhere.

2. My company has been successful internationally for over 20 years. I travel a lot and don't have any problems with people from other cultures.

3. It is most efficient to work in a team with people who are like yourself.

4. We pledge to get rid of unconscious bias in our organization.
5. At last, I've found what I need. There's a great book with cultural dimensions and data for the countries that I work with.
6. I'm a native speaker of English so I'm lucky that I don't have any problems communicating internationally.
7. Face-to-face meetings are obviously better than virtual ones.
8. My door is always open. If a team member has a problem, they just need to come and see me.
9. The others accept my opinion because I am the expert in the team.
10. All managers were sent the circular with the new policy. It has now been implemented globally.
11. I've been there several times on holiday with my family. I'm sure we will have a great time when I start my three-year assignment.
12. When in Rome do as the Romans do.

Suggested answers can be found in the answer key at the back of the book.

Importance of cultural differences

We live in a world of increasing volatility, uncertainty, complexity and ambiguity. The acronym 'VUCA', which originated in the US Army War College in the 1990s, is now widely used beyond the military context to describe the challenges of the twenty-first century. One of the key skills needed to thrive in the VUCA world is intercultural competence.

Globalization means that more people than ever before are coming into contact with cultures other than their own. Technology has created global hyperconnectivity. People are able to travel further, faster and more easily than in the past, the labour force is more mobile and diverse, and there are unprecedented numbers of people trying to escape from poverty, conflicts and natural disasters. Regardless of whether you talk about expats, migrants, refugees or global nomads, it is clear that many people are on the move.

The increase of offshoring, the internationalization of supply chains and global infrastructure projects, such as China's 'New Silk Road' or 'Belt and Road Initiative', are leading to new levels of interdependency. Although globalization has led to a new degree of standardization, national and regional identities are asserting themselves, as is seen by the rise of nationalism in many parts of the world. There are four main areas where culture impacts international business:

1 Business travel

If you travel abroad for business, you inevitably experience cultural differences. For many business travellers this may not be more than a superficial experience. It is perfectly possible to stay in your comfort zone within an international 'bubble' even when you are thousands of miles away from home. You fly to an international airport, stay in a hotel belonging to an international chain, watch TV programmes on the same channels as at home and go to an office in a familiar corporate environment, to have meetings with colleagues who have studied at the same business school as you.

When you wake up in the morning you wonder where you are – the only thing that is different is the light switch on the wrong side of the bed. Even the breakfast buffet is similar, or even better, with noodles and dumplings as well as bacon and eggs, croissants and toast, muesli and porridge, and camel as well as cow's milk. If you taste any local food, it is when you are invited for a meal at a local restaurant. Your culturally aware hosts have selected a place which is popular with international visitors; few, if any, locals are to be seen. You drink cola light and experience zero culture. All this can easily lead you to think that things are the same everywhere. Only when you dig deeper do you find out that this is not always the case.

2 International assignments

Individuals who go on a longer assignment to another country have more contact with local culture, and if your family goes with you then this will be even more intense. The working partner is happy in a familiar setting and stimulated by responsibilities unimaginable in their home country. For the 'trailing spouse' things aren't so easy. They may have given up their career at home and can't get a work permit abroad. Especially if you have children, the non-working partner may well have more contact with locals than you do and will have to deal with shopkeepers, teachers and doctors – all in a foreign language which they are struggling to learn. The dissatisfaction of your spouse or partner can put considerable strains on your relationship and, in extreme cases, lead to premature return. Most international assignments do not fail as dramatically as some of the literature might suggest, but too often the performance of the delegate on an international assignment is under par. It can be exciting to lead a nomadic life, but it can also make you rootless.

3 International teams

Even if you rarely, or never, go on business trips and aren't among the relatively few people who are sent on a long-term delegation abroad, you are nevertheless increasingly likely to have to cope with cultural differences. As a member of a diverse team, you will need intercultural skills to collaborate effectively and be able to do this virtually, as many dispersed teams never, or rarely, meet face-to-face.

4 Going international

More and more people are affected by cross-border business. This ranges from setting up sales or offshore production facilities in different countries to being involved in joint-ventures or mergers and acquisitions. Under pressure to get things done quickly the culture factor is often neglected. The consequences are strained relationships, lost time and an escalation of costs.

There are many examples of failure to take cultural factors into account leading to loss of money and even lives. Barmeyer and Franklin (2016) describe how the Swedish furniture maker IKEA faced hefty criticism from Swedish customers when it produced a catalogue for the Arab world, with women airbrushed out of the pictures. Hammerich and Lewis (2013) show how the US retailer Walmart, which had been highly successful in the USA, tried to expand into Europe via Germany but had to withdraw after a few years. It lacked knowledge of work regulations and failed to take into account the behaviour of local customers. 'Baggers' at the cash tills to pack customers' shopping, while expected in the USA, were looked on with suspicion by German shoppers. The 'three-foot rule', under which a shop worker had to ask the customer if they wanted any help if they approached them closer than three feet, was considered to be irritating rather than helpful. Employees objected to the morning warm-up workouts chanting the company song.

The sophisticated world of high tech is not exempt from cultural errors. In 1999 NASA's $125 million Mars Climate Orbiter was lost in space because engineers failed to make a simple conversion from imperial/US customary units to metric units. Another infamous example is the crash of Asiana Airlines Flight 214 in 2013, one of a series of tragic accidents involving Korean planes. *The Guardian* (2014) reported that the pilot was being trained to fly the 777 and didn't think he had the authority to abort the flight. 'Among the other issues raised by the investigation are some that long have concerned aviation officials, including hesitancy by some pilots to abort a landing when things go awry or to challenge a captain's actions.' At that time many of the pilots had a military background, and Korean culture tends to favour steep hierarchies.

Culture and functions

Many books on intercultural business are for managers, and in the first wave of globalization they were the people at the forefront of coping with cultural differences. Of course, they still are, but it is time to shift the focus away from the jet-setting global executive and look more closely at the influence of cultural differences on people working in many other functions which are just as vital for business success.

Marketing

Marketing is perhaps the most obvious and celebrated area where cultural differences can have a major impact. Future demand for products and services is likely to increase most in China, India, Sub-Saharan Africa and Latin America as new middle classes emerge in these regions. To access these markets, businesses will need to understand the cultural differences which influence products, price, place and promotion.

Food for thought is provided by McDonald's. While, of course, one of its strengths is that its products and processes are highly standardized, it has adapted to local demands. Spicy Wings are served in Beijing, McHuevo burgers in Montevideo, kosher Big Macs in Jerusalem and vegetarian McMaharajah burgers in Delhi. To be accepted in the Saudi Arabian market Starbucks even adapted its famous logo from the female siren figure to a crown.

An exclusive milliner in Munich found that customers from different cultures reacted very differently to the prices of her hand-made hats. While most locals wanted the highest quality for the lowest price, wealthy tourists from Russia looked at the most expensive hats on display first. They want to show their new-found wealth by wearing high-status fashion items.

At the beginning of the twenty-first century computer tomography scanners used by hospitals in Europe and the USA were considered to be too expensive and overengineered for use in regional hospitals in China. The European manufacturer realized that the equipment had to be adapted if it was to have a chance of being adopted in this market. 'Culture-oriented usability' means adapting the functionality to local needs.

Human resources (HR)

HR professionals are on the front line in the global 'war for talent'. Demand for specialist staff and demographic changes mean that there is a worldwide shortage of skilled labour. It seems that the talents are winning the war.

'They don't even bother to send a photo or provide basic facts like their date of birth in their application,' complained a German HR manager, who at the same time was faced with a lack of applicants from the USA for top talent positions. What they had failed to take into account was that in the USA you don't reveal your age, racial background and gender in a job application.

Retention is just as important. Western companies operating in China are hiring young Chinese and training them up for the job, only to find that the new recruits leave after a short time to work for a local competitor. The costs include the recruiting process, onboarding and training, the time lost in finding a successor and the potential loss of valuable knowledge to the competitor. HR managers have to face the challenge of designing contracts which incentivize people to stay.

Compensation policies need to function globally while respecting local differences. This involves taking into account costs of living, tax systems, exchange rates, inflation and the expectations of employees. Even the amount of holiday employees are entitled to varies widely across the world.

Finance

Finance teams are faced with collecting data from colleagues and auditing at different sites around the world. This involves being able to get people to do things they don't want to do. It may not be enough just to send a quick text or email. People from some cultures will act only if they know why they are providing the figures and feel that they can trust their colleague. To overcome resistance and get the information they need, auditors will require a range of influencing skills which produce results among different people in different contexts.

Procurement

Those involved in procurement in internationally active companies frequently have to deal with people from many different countries within the course of one day at work. Alongside knowledge of markets and laws, they will need to be able to communicate effectively in internationally understandable English and have culturally appropriate negotiating skills.

Production

As multicultural workforces become increasingly common, production managers have to deal with employees from very different backgrounds. The supervisor is challenged by the multicultural employees on the production line. They ask questions like: What are the workers talking about when they speak to each other in their own language? How do I cope with the holiday requests when they all want to return to their home country in the summer? How can I accommodate different national and religious holidays? Do I really have to stop the production line for a prayer break?

Engineering

Service and installation engineers in internationally active companies will often have to travel to many very different countries and work under high pressure in extreme conditions. On site they will be collaborating with local management and technical staff who may have had little exposure to other cultures.

Software architecture

Software architects frequently work in international teams. The focus on solving the problem in hand and their respect for the specialist knowledge foster effective collaboration. Many different nationalities may be bound together laughing at references to 1970s cult novel *The Hitchhiker's Guide to the Galaxy* but struggle to deal with clients from HR or Sales when developing software for personnel processes or customer relationship management. Requirements' engineering doesn't just demand technical expertise but also a high degree of empathy for your client.

Environment, health and safety (EHS)

Attitudes to both following rules and regulations and to quality vary widely. In one culture a rule may be seen as a guideline and how far you follow the guidelines will depend on the circumstances. In other cultures, rules are followed regardless of the situation. These fundamental differences can have serious consequences when people from two or more types of culture meet.

There are all too many accidents on building sites around the world where the health and safety standards are designed by people who lack knowledge of the local conditions. Safety boots are provided for the workers who then give them to family members. Rules are in a language that locals don't understand. Chinese men reject green safety helmets as they don't want to be seen 'wearing a green hat', as traditionally the husbands of prostitutes were forced to wear green hats. An Italian car manufacturer found that workers were not wearing the safety glasses provided and only overcame the resistance by providing glasses with a cool design.

Shipping

Shipping is one of the most globalized industries, with about 80 per cent of world trade conducted by sea. A ship can be owned in one country, have cargo from another and be run by a multicultural crew. The crew have to function efficiently in a highly stressful environment, working in all weathers, with tight deadlines, poor conditions and a heavy workload. They spend long periods of time away from their friends and families, share their living quarters with crew members from many different places, and may even lack a common language. Progoulaki and Theotokas (2016) describe managing diverse crews effectively as a 'key competence for shipping companies'.

IT

Alongside their technical skills, IT managers and teams need considerable intercultural awareness. They have to be aware of different technical standards across the world and, if standardizing systems globally, will have to persuade people with different cultural backgrounds to adopt the technology. They deal with a range of internal clients and external suppliers.

Corporate communications

Corporate communications experts in international companies have to produce material that is appropriate for internal and external audiences. It is challenging to find a style that suits everybody while not diluting the corporate brand. Even when producing something as apparently simple as an in-house company newsletter, cultural preferences have to be taken into account. While some employees may expect detail, others prefer 'the big picture'. In hierarchical cultures it may be more appropriate to have features about top management than in cultures with flatter hierarchies.

Team assistance

The job of the team assistant has changed radically over the past 20 years. As well as traditional office and interpersonal skills, modern team and management assistants now need to have a high level of IT, language and project management skills. In their unique position at the interface between customers and suppliers, management and staff face considerable pressures from all sides, juggling conflicting interests while being expected to take initiative, be highly efficient and diplomatic, and remain calm and polite at all times. Although they may be in the back office, they are at the front line of intercultural encounters.

Medical services

Company medical services provide support to business travellers and delegates on foreign assignments. This requires not only up-to-date knowledge of the medical situation in different countries but also an awareness of stress-related issues. If they are treating employees from other cultures, they need to know how to relate to them effectively. How people see and express pain and what they expect from doctors varies widely.

Culture

What exactly do we mean by the term 'culture' in a business context? In this book 'culture' is not primarily used in the sense of literature, music and art, but as *a shared system of attitudes, beliefs, meanings, values and behaviour.* It is what Hofstede et al. (2010) called 'collective mental programming' or the 'software of the mind' or simply 'the way we do things around here'.

Various metaphors have been used for culture. One of the most popular images is the iceberg. While it can be helpful to illustrate that tangible expressions of culture, such as behaviour, clothes and food, are above and the underlying attitudes, beliefs and values are below the surface of the water, it is too static an image to reflect the dynamic and fluid nature of culture. Ideas such as monolithic blocks of culture clashing against one another or that we are all on the *Titanic* waiting to crash into the cultural iceberg are simply too dramatic.

Bolten (2018) prefers to talk about 'fuzzy cultures', and interculturalists replace the overexposed iceberg image with others: the hippopotamus half-submerged in the water, mosaics, brush strokes in an Impressionist painting, the Möbius strip or the Kota masks of Gabon.

The **tree model** contrasts visible and hidden culture, with the roots standing for the historical origins of culture. This metaphor can be extended to global mobility. Moving between cultures is like transplanting a tree. To be successful the roots have to be protected and support is needed in the new environment. Like people, not all trees are the same. Some people have deep roots and are hard to move, while others are like plants or shrubs which can be replanted in different places as long as the conditions are right.

The **onion model** (Figure 1.1) shows layers of culture which can be peeled away to reveal underlying basic assumptions. It has been adapted from the 'three levels of culture' by Schein (2017):

1. **artifacts:** objects, visible structures, processes and observed behaviour

2. **beliefs and values:** ideals, goals and ideologies

3. **assumptions:** unconscious beliefs and values which drive thought, feeling and behaviour.

Onion model

ASSUMPTIONS

BELIEFS & VALUES

ARTIFACTS

Figure 1.1 The onion model of culture

Culture at work

Much of the research into culture has focused on national cultures, but other types of group identity can be just as, or more, important. To be successful across cultures it helps to step back and take on the role of an anthropologist observing as neutrally as possible how people work and what influences them. Figure 1.2 shows some different types of cultural influence in the workplace.

Figure 1.2 Cultures at work

Each of the elements shown in the diagram influences our behaviour:

- **Sector.** The cultures of different industries and sectors shape how people working in them think and act. Building a power station is different from auditing a company, developing a new medicine or managing an international hotel chain. Installing and maintaining wind turbines is different from trading cryptocurrencies. The products and processes as well as the environment in which people work influence how they think and behave.

- **Corporate.** Every company has its own corporate culture, even if not everyone is always conscious of it. You can find out more about it by applying the onion model. Start by looking at the artifacts, such as the corporate website or annual report. What things are mentioned in the vision and mission statements? What sort of people feature in the photographs? Do they stress sustainability or profit? What does the company claim to be its values? How are you greeted when you visit its offices? Who attends and speaks most in meetings? Which assumptions underlie these values?

- **Profession.** There are clear professional cultures. As professions require considerable education and training, it is not surprising that this intensive experience can influence the people who later work in that profession. This is reflected in the numerous popular stereotypes for different professions such as the 'geek' or 'nerd' for IT specialists or 'bean counter' for accountants.

- **Site.** It is striking to see different cultures develop at different locations or sites across the world or also within the same country, region or town. The HQ often has a different culture from that of regional offices.

- **Team.** Teams develop their own cultures. Some aspects to think about are: How do they communicate and collaborate? Who makes decisions? What rituals do they have? How do they celebrate team or personal success?

- **Department.** Departments and business units within a company have their own cultures, influenced by the environment in which they work and the styles of the people who work there. Many issues arise from 'silo thinking' within a company. Clashes between the silos can have even more impact than national cultural clash.

- **Position.** Managers will be subject to different influences from those working on the production line, and there may be a lack of contact between people from these different position levels. Blue-collar workers complain that the management is out of touch. The middle management beautify project reports when presenting results to the top. Top management complain that middle managers are blocking change. Even where there is open-plan office space, hierarchical zones form.

- **Function.** Functions and roles are also important. Often, people with similar functions identify with others with the same function, and so form a subculture. They may drink tea or coffee or go for lunch together and share experiences, even if they are from different national cultures.

- **Length of service.** How long has someone been in your company? The culture of the 'old hands' can be very different from that of the 'newbies'.

Multiple cultural identities

A trend in the intercultural field is to recognize how important it is to accept that it is important not just to talk about national cultures. 'We are all Michelin men,' says Rathje (2009). We all have multiple cultural identities, like the rings on the iconic symbol of the famous tyre maker. Rathje calls this 'multicollectivity'. How important each of these different identities is depends on the situation we find ourselves in; the identities are not static but change over time. Here is an example of the multiple cultural identities of one person:

- female
- daughter, sister, wife
- friend
- colleague
- Generation X (born 1965–1976)
- university graduate
- engineer

- employee of an international company with HQ in the UK
- Chinese nationality
- resident of Beijing
- enthusiastic cook
- fan of British football team Manchester United.

When at home with her family in China her identity as a daughter or sister is most important. She feels a strong sense of being Chinese when she celebrates Chinese New Year with her family and friends in Beijing. When on a business trip to company HQ in the UK her identity as an engineer is at the forefront. Her support for the Manchester United football team bonds her with her British colleagues in the pub after work. She identifies as a cook when she shares recipes in a WeChat community. She reserves her most private and intimate world for her husband.

Exercise 1.2

Make a list of your cultural identities. Compare your list with those of your colleagues. You may be surprised to discover you share some common identities that you were not previously aware of.

Going further

Hammerich, K. and Lewis, R. D. (2013) *Fish Can't See Water: How National Culture can Make or Break Your Corporate Strategy*, Chichester: John Wiley.
A look at the influence of national cultures on global companies with real-life business cases and a framework for analysing corporate culture.
Van Boeijen, A. and Zijlstra, Y. (2020) *Culture Sensitive Design: A Guide to Culture in Practice*, Amsterdam: BIS Publishers.
A beautiful and informative book about the influence of culture on design.

2

Globality Check

Intercultural Competence

The stranger sees only what he knows.

African proverb

Key questions

- How fit are you to work across cultures?
- What does it mean to be interculturally competent?

Before looking in more detail at what intercultural competence really is, take some time out to reflect on your own intercultural skills with the help of the Globality check.

Globality check

This quick self-assessment helps you to reflect on your experience, attitudes and knowledge, as well as on your ability to see things from different perspectives and analyse situations in which cultural factors play a role. Suggested answers can be found in the answer key at the back of the book.

Experience

> ### Exercise 2.1
> Think about situations at work or in your private life when you experienced cultural differences. What happened and what did you learn?

Attitudes

> ### Exercise 2.2
> Which of the following apply to you?
>
> Rate each of these statements on a scale of 1–5, where 1 means 'not true at all' and 5 is 'completely true'.
> 1. I am interested in foreign cultures.
> 2. I am able to speak several languages.
> 3. I can communicate effectively.
> 4. I am a good listener.
> 5. I observe carefully what is going on before interpreting other people's behaviour.
> 6. I reflect regularly on the effects of my own behaviour and can adapt where necessary.
> 7. I try to respect the views of other people even if I don't agree with them.
> 8. I thrive on complexity and ambiguity
> 9. I see diverse teams as a potential source of innovation.

Knowledge

> ### Exercise 2.3
> As well as having the right attitude it is also important to have relevant knowledge about cultural differences. Start by thinking about some basic things you know about other cultures.

1. List as many different ways of greeting people that you can think of in different cultures.
2. What different eating habits have you experienced in different cultures in a business context?
3. What different kinds of business clothing have you seen when on trips around the world?

Perspectives

Exercise 2.4

Different people perceive and interpret things in different ways. This exercise helps you to think about things from different perspectives. You see the glass as half empty or half full or you think about its weight. Culturally competent people are able to see multiple perspectives.

How can the following phrases be interpreted positively and negatively?
Example: 'Hi. How are you doing?' Positive: Informality; Negative: Disrespect
1. No risk. No fun.
2. There's no time for small talk.
3. Time is money.
4. When the going gets tough, the tough get going.
5. It was just a joke.
6. Do your own thing.
7. Every cloud has a silver lining.
8. What's your bottom line?

Skills

Case: The battery factory

Exercise 2.5

What cultural issues do you think might play a role in this case?

What actions would you recommend to make the project a success?

A CEO from country A has asked for your advice. Their company has been highly successful in their home market but the management team has little international experience. They have taken advantage of government subsidies to build a factory for the production of batteries for electric cars on a greenfield site in country B. The site, just outside a town with a population of 30,000, is well connected by road and rail to their main customers. They plan to bring 300 technical experts and managers from country A and to hire about 1,500 local employees for a wide range of positions.

Intercultural competence

For many years intelligence has been measured using the intelligence quotient (IQ). Goleman (1995) talks about emotional intelligence (EQ), and with the increasing recognition of the importance of intercultural skills, Earley and Ang (2003) speak of 'cultural intelligence', or CQ. The Organisation for Economic Co-operation and Development's Programme for International Student Assessment (PISA), which compares young people's performances in countries around the world, has added 'global competence' to what it tests, alongside mathematics, science and reading skills. They define global competence as 'the capacity to examine local, global and intercultural issues, to understand and appreciate the perspectives and world views of others, to engage in open, appropriate and effective interactions with people from different cultures, and to act for collective well-being and sustainable development'.

Intercultural business competence

In the context of business, intercultural competence can be defined as the knowledge, skills and attitudes you need to create value for your business from cultural differences. Employees who display intercultural business competence overcome cultural barriers and build constructive relationships with partners from different cultures for mutual benefit; they are able to leverage diversity for competitive advantage.

Typically they:

- are curious to find out about other cultures

- show a spirit of humble enquiry

- are keen to learn languages

- communicate effectively in a culturally appropriate way

- have knowledge about cultures which is relevant for international business

- can reflect critically on their own culturally determined attitudes, beliefs and behaviour

- understand the culturally determined behaviour of colleagues and business partners

- can adapt their own behaviour as appropriate

- show respect for and empathize with colleagues and partners from different cultures

- are able to cope with ambiguity and complexity

- make use of the intercultural potential in teams and turn it into a competitive advantage

- have resilience for dealing with conflicts without losing sight of their own position.

Levels of intercultural competence

There are broadly four levels of any competence. Think about learning to drive a car. As a child you see adults driving but you don't understand what it means to drive and you can't drive. This is known as *unconscious incompetence*. Later you decide that you want to drive, realize that you can't and will have to take lessons. This is *conscious incompetence*. Even after you have passed your driving test you can drive but may still have to think about what you are doing when you are driving. This is called *conscious competence*. The final stage is when you have driven for some time and you start to drive automatically. This is called *unconscious competence*. This cycle can repeat itself. If you want to start driving Formula One cars then you will need to do additional training.

These principles can be applied to intercultural competence. Bennett (1993) describes six positions on a continuum between *ethnocentrism* and *ethnorelativism*. Ethnocentrism is 'the experience of one's own culture as central to reality', while ethnorelativism is 'the experience of one's own and other cultures as relative to context'. The six positions in his continuum are: denial, defence, minimization, acceptance, adaptation and integration. Figure 2.1 shows a simplified model with five levels. The individual accepts, understands, adapts to, functions in and bridges cultures.

At the lowest level, people recognize that cultural norms other than their own exist. At the level of understanding, people are aware of differences in values, attitudes and behaviour and try to think about where they come from. When people adapt, they start to change their own behaviour to fit into the culture of others. Someone who functions across cultures will work effectively with people who are different from themselves. DiStefano et al. (2005) describe bridging cultures as 'an attempt to minimize differences by understanding the frame of reference of others ... The word "bridging" is more than just understanding differences between people; it is

Levels of intercultural competence

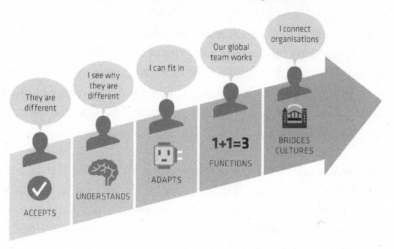

Figure 2.1 Levels of intercultural competence

about overcoming the obstacle of differences between people and crossing over to the "other" side.' People who bridge culture gaps actively support collaboration between people by consciously using their experience and knowledge of cultural differences to reach a common target.

Intercultural competence assessment

The Globality check aims to stimulate your thinking about your intercultural competence. If you or your team want to go deeper, you can consider taking a commercially available test. Over 100 intercultural assessment tools are currently available, so it can be hard to choose which one is best. There are basically two types of test. Some aim to assess intercultural competence in general, while others try to identify a person's preferred cultural preferences and map them against the cultural dimensions of a specific culture. Some are closely linked to courses offered by training providers;

they compare your cultural preferences with those of the target culture and suggest ways of coping with the differences.

Here is a selection of a few of these tools. When deciding which one to use, think about not only the costs but also what exactly you want to use it for, how relevant the questions are for your target group, and which languages you need it to be available in; check the technical requirements to make sure that the users can easily access the test.

- **International Development Inventory (IDI).** The IDI is based on Milton Bennett's Developmental Model of Intercultural Sensitivity. It is designed for personal development and self-awareness, audience analysis, organizational development and intercultural training. The IDI generates a profile of an individual's or group's predominant stage of development.

- **Intercultural Readiness Check (IRC).** The IRC is designed to assess participants in four competences: intercultural sensitivity, intercultural communication, building commitment and managing uncertainty. Brinkmann and Van Weerdenburg (2014) put the IRC into a broader context of 'intercultural readiness'.

- **International Profiler (TIP).** World Work's TIP is a questionnaire and feedback tool designed to help managers and professionals understand where they typically put the emphasis when working internationally. It helps to raise their awareness of potential areas in which they may require future development, and suggests actions they can take to fill the gaps.

- **Cultural Orientations Indicator® COI®.** The COI assesses a user's work style and cultural preferences. The resulting recommendations can serve to bridge cultural gaps, leading to strengthened business relationships and successful initiatives. The assessment is organized into three dimensions: Interaction Style, Thinking Style and Sense of Self. It is part of the Cultural Navigator® learning platform which provides culture-specific information. Putz et al. (2014) describe how it can be used.

- **GlobeSmart®.** A tool which enables you to compare the preferences of yourself and your team with culture-specific information on over a hundred countries. It is provided by Aperian Global®.

If you are planning to use these tools with people from various cultures, check first how acceptable they are to the target group. Attitudes to testing vary widely. If you integrate measurement of intercultural sensitivity into assessment or development centres, make sure you involve professionals from the target cultures, either as part of the selection panel or as observers. They are in the best position to evaluate the behaviour and performance of the candidates and decide how culturally appropriate it is.

Going further

Brinkmann, U. and Van Weerdenburg, O. (2014) *Intercultural Readiness: Four Competences for Working Across Cultures*, Houndmills: Palgrave Macmillan.
A practical model for assessing and developing intercultural competences for work.
Caligiuri, P. (2021) *Build Your Cultural Agility: The Nine Competencies of Successful Global Professionals*, London: Kogan Page.
A practical guide to self-, relationship- and task-management competencies which make up 'cultural agility'.

3

Return on Diversity

The Power of Difference

A lot of different flowers make a bouquet.

Islamic proverb

Key questions

- Why is diversity important for international business?
- Which types of diversity do you need to consider in your workplace?

Diversity is big business. Diversity, equity, inclusion and belonging (DEIB) are no longer considered to be 'nice to have' but are 'need to have', with more and more companies appointing chief diversity officers, who set ambitious targets, launch initiatives and run company-wide training programmes. Vociferous critics are less enthusiastic and doubt whether all this activity and investment have really changed anything; others reject diversity initiatives altogether. This chapter explores the business case for promoting diversity and inclusion in organizations.

Business case for diversity

It helps to start by thinking about the natural world and agriculture. Farmers may be tempted to grow a single crop to benefit from economies of scale. The disadvantage is that, if the crop fails, they lose everything. A classic example of this is the banana. Most of the world is heavily dependent on seedless Cavendish bananas, which are under threat from the fungal disease Fusarium wilt. If this disease spreads, bananas will be in extremely short supply. What is happening here is in stark contrast to what happens in nature. Sustainability in the natural world is based on biodiversity; in a tropical rain forest there are many different species, and if one species dies out, the forest lives on.

The same principle applies to business. If you employ only one type of person, focus on one type of customer and rely on one type of supplier, and offer a limited range of services or products, while you may be successful in the short term, your company will not survive in the long run in a fast-changing business environment. It is quite simple: you need to embrace diversity if you want to survive in the VUCA world.

Research led by Catalyst has identified '39 reasons why diversity matters'. The four main areas it identifies are: improving financial performance, leveraging talent, reflecting the marketplace, and increasing innovation.

Complying with regulations

In many countries there are strict laws about diversity and discrimination. To get contracts and avoid costly lawsuits and reputational damage it is essential that you comply with relevant diversity legislation.

An example of businesses having to prove that they have implemented a diversity policy in order to be considered as a bidder for a contract is the London Organising Committee of the Olympic Games and Paralympic Games (LOCOG) for London 2012. LOCOG had a clear policy of using a diverse pool of suppliers. This was relatively successful, with 18 per cent of UK companies involved run by ethnic minority groups, 20 per cent run by women, 1.7 per cent run by owners with a disability, and 2 per cent by members of the LGBT+ community.

Innovating

Digitalization, connectivity and deregulation are creating the need for rapid innovation. Although monocultural teams may be able to function more quickly than multicultural ones, they are less likely to be as innovative. It is not by chance that the teams of scientists which developed the vaccines for COVID-19 in record time were all diverse. There is a clear relationship between the diversity of companies' management teams and the revenues they get from innovative products and services. Johansson (2004) shows how innovation happens at the 'intersection' where 'ideas and concepts from diverse industries, cultures, and disciplines meet'.

Staying close to customers

If you want to understand how diverse customer groups think and market your products and services successfully, then you obviously need to involve people from the target group. If you don't do this, mistakes can be expensive. An advertising campaign in China for an Italian luxury fashion brand which showed a Chinese woman struggling to eat spaghetti with chopsticks is an example of how a brand can be severely damaged overnight; more involvement of the target group in marketing could have saved the day. Increasingly, customers expect the business they buy from to reflect their diversity. Advertising with sexist or racist content can have disastrous effects.

Hiring and retaining talent

There is a serious shortage of talent worldwide for skilled workers, particularly those with a background in STEM (Science, Technology, Engineering and Mathematics). This means that employers simply cannot afford to exclude potential candidates on the basis of their gender, physical ability, sexual orientation, ethnic background or any other diversity dimension.

Too often companies focus on recruiting but neglect retention. If you are to retain employees from diverse backgrounds, they need to feel that they belong and can develop. If employees perceive that this isn't the case, they will leave. Your investment of time, energy and money in hiring and onboarding them will be lost.

Avoiding the pain of exclusion

Researchers in the USA have examined the effect of exclusion on the brain. Eisenberger (2012) simulated social exclusion by asking subjects to play a computer game called Cyberball. Some were excluded from the game without warning. Others were asked to view a picture of a person who recently rejected them and to think back to the experience of rejection. Using neuroimaging techniques, the reactions of their brain were compared to what happened when they experienced physical pain, simulated by subjecting them to painful heat.

The reactions of the brain were remarkably similar in both cases, suggesting that, as far as the brain is concerned, there is little difference between physical and social pain. Eisenberger concludes:

> Experiences of social exclusion or relationship loss may be just as emotionally distressing as experiences of physical pain. Although physical pain is typically regarded as more serious or objectively distressing because it has a clear biological basis, the work reviewed here demonstrates that social pain could be argued to be just as distressing because it activates the same underlying neural machinery.

This has wide-reaching implications for society as well as for teams. If a member of your team feels the pain of exclusion, their performance will suffer.

Diversity dimensions

According to the *Cambridge Dictionary* diversity is 'a range of different things or people'. The Wheel of Difference (Figure 3.1), which is based on the work of Gardenswartz and Rowe (2003), shows some key diversity dimensions. At the centre of the wheel is the individual's personality: every human being is different and unique. Then come inner diversity dimensions, which are fixed or can only be changed to a limited extent. They include age, gender, sexual orientation, race and ethnicity, and national origin as well as physical and mental ability. The outer dimensions include religion, education, family status, socio-economic status, political views, appearance, region and location. These are not fixed and they change over time. The organizational dimensions are the influences connected to the workplace such as corporate and professional cultures (see Chapter 1). Although many people focus on gender and race, any of these dimensions can be the basis of bias or discrimination. For instance, someone from a particular school or college may find they have advantages over others: single mothers are often not considered for promotion; membership of a trade union or political party can be seen negatively by employers; people can be judged by their weight, their tattoos, their voice or their regional accent.

Which diversity dimensions are considered to be relevant will vary depending on where you are in the world. In many parts of the African continent tribal identity will be important, while in the USA the military experience of veterans is often included. We clearly need a diverse approach to diversity itself.

Age

People of a similar age share certain experiences which are connected with their generation. They have all experienced a period of conflict or peace, poverty or prosperity or technological change which binds them together. This can set them apart from people from other generations and be a cause of positive or negative discrimination. Talk is of Baby Boomers, Millennials or Gen Y and Gen Z, each with their own characteristics. Even these terms are culturally bound: for example, not everyone experienced the post-Second World War 'baby boom'.

Wheel of difference

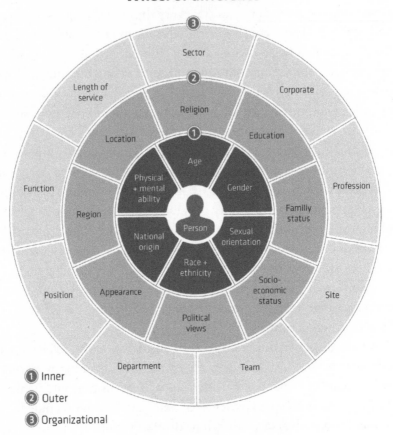

Figure 3.1 The Wheel of Difference
Figure based on concept developed by Gardenswartz & Rowe, https://www. gardenswartzrowe.com/why-g-r

China is a good example of how important the generational factor can be. The country has gone through massive changes in the last 80 years. To understand the Chinese people you meet it helps to think about the historical events or state policies that may have helped shape the environment in which they grew up. Was it the Cultural Revolution (1966–76), the one-child policy (1980–2016) or the unprecedentedly fast economic growth that has taken place since the 1980s? A powerful illustration of the breathtaking speed of this last change is the fact that China used more cement between 2011 and 2013 than the USA did in the entire twentieth century. Guides to China often say that the Chinese are 'collective' because they work on the rice fields. How far can this really be true of a generation which has grown up as only children in the concrete jungle of the megacities?

Gender and sexual orientation

In the heated debates about gender, it is important to be clear about the terminology. There are differences between the terms 'gender', 'gender identity' and 'sexual orientation'. *Assigned gender* is the sex initially given to someone at birth. *Gender identity* is the gender with which an individual identifies. *Sexual orientation* is a term used to describe whom you are attracted to. It includes attraction to the same gender (homosexuality), a gender different from your own (heterosexuality), both men and women (bisexuality), all genders (pansexuality) or neither (asexuality). The acronym LGBT+ stands for lesbian, gay, bisexual, transgender and related communities.

Race and ethnicity

The terms 'race' and 'ethnicity' are also the subject of considerable discussion, and different historical developments mean that they are understood differently by people from different cultures. This can be illustrated by how they are seen in the USA and Germany.

Bryce (2020) quotes Nina Jablonski from Pennsylvania State University who says that 'race is understood by most people as a mixture of physical, behavioural and cultural attributes. Ethnicity recognizes differences between people mostly on the basis of language and shared culture.' People can have several ethnic identities: 'Some might choose to identify themselves as Asian American, British Somali or an Ashkenazi Jew, for instance, drawing on different aspects of their ascribed racial identity, culture, ancestry and religion.'

In Germany the term 'race' has been avoided for many years because of its association with the discredited racial theories on which Nazi ideology was based. As the country becomes more multicultural, there is more discussion about racism. Elger (2020) quotes Yasemin Shooman, the scientific director of the Centre for Integration and Migration Research, who comments:

> In Germany, racism and anti-Semitism were considered historical phenomena for far too long … The concept of race is taboo due to the crimes of National Socialists … Just because there is no longer talk of 'races', that doesn't mean racism has disappeared. Nowadays, arguments aren't based on biological race theories but on ethnic, cultural or even religious affiliation. The purpose, however, is still to exclude groups deemed 'foreign' from access to material and symbolic resources as well as to legitimize the privileged status of one's own group.

National origin

This refers to the nationality of your birth. Of course, your nationality can change as a result of migration, and in some cases people have multiple nationalities.

Physical and mental ability

Many different types of physical and mental ability also need to be considered. While some types can be seen – for instance, if someone is a wheelchair user – others are not immediately obvious at first sight. This is particularly true of cognitive diversity.

Neurodiversity refers to people who think differently from the norms in society and includes those with autism, Asperger's, dyslexia and attention deficit hyperactivity disorder (ADHD). People with these conditions have often faced discrimination in the workplace, but now many companies are realizing their potential.

Some neurodiverse individuals are particularly good at coding and AI programming, where there is a worldwide shortage of talent. Taylor (2021) reports how the consultancy company EY has even set up a Neurodiversity Centre of Excellence to tap into the talents of neurodiverse individuals globally. There have already been concrete positive results, for example the development of a COVID-19 tracker which assesses the impact of the disease on clients. As Taylor (2012) says: 'It tracks experience against our initial expectation and runs scenarios about what impacts will be. It's been incredibly helpful, and we believe it has impacted the firm in the range of $300 million – $500 million.'

Diversity, equity, inclusion and belonging (DEIB)

There are subtle but significant differences in these terms. The illustration inspired by an idea from the Robert Wood Johnson Foundation shows the difference between *equality* and *equity*. Treating everyone equally (equality) is not the same as creating equal opportunities (equity).

Equality and Equity

EQUALITY

EQUITY

Figure 3.2 Equality and equity
Figure based on concept developed by Robert Wood Johnson Foundation, 2017 https://www.rwjf.org/en/library/infographics/visualizing-health-equity.html

Diversity is the existence of multiple identities, while *inclusion* means that the different perspectives of all individuals matter so that people feel a sense of *belonging*. A concrete way of describing the difference between diversity and inclusion is, as the US activist Verna Myers said: 'Diversity is being invited to the party, inclusion is being asked to dance.' Arthur Chan, quoted in Robbins (2021), sums up the difference between the terms when he says: 'Diversity is a fact; Equity is a choice; Inclusion is an action; Belonging is an outcome.'

From exclusion to inclusion

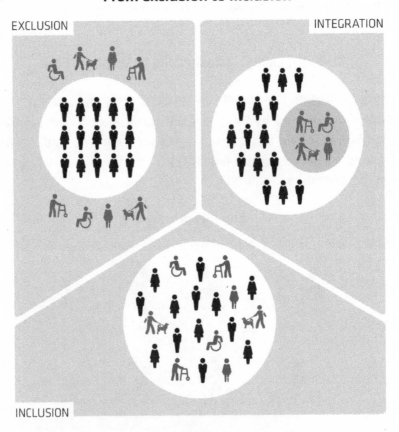

Figure 3.3 From exclusion to inclusion
Figure based on on concept developed by So'Lille association (Solidarité Lilloise Etudiante) https://lepole.education/en/pedagogical-culture/63-the-in-clusive-school.html?start=1

Societies and organizations vary widely in how they treat diverse groups of people. For many years the term 'melting pot' was widely used in the USA to refer to the cultural assimilation of immigrants. More recently, this has been replaced with other metaphors of a multicultural society like 'salad bowl' or 'kaleidoscope' which show that cultures mix but still remain distinct. Three different ways of treating diversity are illustrated in the diagram based on an idea by the So'Lille Association.

- **Exclusion:** people from particular groups are prevented from being active in the organization.

- **Integration:** individuals from particular groups can be active in the organization, as members of a distinct minority.

- **Inclusion:** individuals from particular groups can take full part in the organization, with the same rights, access and choices as everyone else.

Creating inclusive organizations

Some people argue that diversity can't be managed. However, just as we can't manage nature but we can farm, so in order to grow a business, we can create inclusive teams and organizations from diversity. Promoting and supporting diversity in the workplace is about valuing everyone in that organization so that everyone feels able to participate fully and achieve their full potential. This is not only a moral obligation but also makes business sense.

Even some of those who believe in the importance of DEIB are beginning to show 'diversity fatigue', frustrated that things are not changing fast enough. For instance, despite massive investment in diversity measures, less than five per cent of leadership roles in US companies are occupied by Black Americans (who account for more than 13 per cent of the population). A major reason for this is that discrimination has deep, systemic roots.

Payne and Kaminstein (2021) describe how some organizations resist more diversity. They identify four ways that organizations do this, what they call 'diversity dodges'. First, training is used more as 'window dressing' rather than as a driver of sustainable change. Second, although there is a designated head of diversity, too often they have to combine their diversity role with other responsibilities and are not given enough power to bring about real change. The third 'dodge' is limited commitment across the whole organization: 'without the active participation, support and commitment of the C-suite in particular, efforts from an office of diversity and inclusion will be constrained, not sustained, cross-company.' Finally, people use the excuse that there are not enough applicants from particular groups; hiring managers claim that they want to hire and promote more Black people or women but can't find suitable candidates. Payne and Kaminstein (2021) advocate setting 'radical hiring targets', 'promoting diversity hiring as a strategy to strengthen the organisation' and considering 'retention to be as critical as hiring'.

Charta der Vielfalt (Diversity Charter) is a non-profit organization in Germany which promotes diversity. It recommends a five-step approach to increasing diversity in organizations whether they be SMEs, larger corporations or public sector bodies:

1. Define objectives

2. Determine current situation

3. Plan implementation

4. Carry our implementation

5. Measure success

High-level questions which need to be asked are:

• How and where can diversity management be helpful for your business, for instance regarding customers and clients, suppliers or business partnerships?

- How are the workforce, the customers and the supplier companies composed?

- What diversity measures already exist without organizations being aware of them?

- How can diversity be introduced or strengthened in an organization?

- What steps lead to the goal?

- In what timeframe is it intended to implement specific measures?

- How are these communicated in the company?

- What effect have the measures had?

- How can each of them be optimized, stopped or expanded to other areas?

Diversity audits and benchmarking

Organizations need to base their DEIB strategy around a clear policy and have ways of measuring progress. This includes having clear business conduct guidelines and regularly carrying out diversity audits and benchmarking. It is important not only to formulate diversity policies or business conduct guidelines but also to make sure that they are living documents. Communicate the guidelines to all employees and make sure breaches of the regulations are addressed. Review and update them regularly.

The principle of 'If you can't measure it, you can't manage it' can also be applied to diversity management. It is important to audit the diversity of your organization. This may be difficult, as the data on all diversity dimensions will not be available, but some attempt needs to be made. When even simple data about the gender of different levels of management is looked at people are often shocked. You have to be prepared to reveal the elephant in the room. Employee engagement surveys need to ask employees how far they perceive that they are working for a diverse organization and how included they feel.

The leading consulting companies have developed tools for diversity audits and carry out benchmarking. The Centre for Global Inclusion has identified 14 categories for benchmarking diversity and inclusion: vision, leadership, structure, recruitment and development, benefits, compensation, learning, assessments, communications, sustainability, social responsibility, products and services, marketing and supplier diversity (O'Mara et al., 2021).

Global diversity initiatives

Just as international companies may have a standard compliance or corporate responsibility policy globally, so many are also seeking to standardize DEIB. As always when it comes to international business, the fundamental challenge is to balance keeping to standards worldwide with acknowledging local cultural contexts.

Kelly (2021) identifies 'opportunities for companies to step up and live their values while expanding internationally'. One is to choose office locations that align with your DEIB values. Kelly describes how, while working as Vice President of Localization at HubSpot, the company chose Colombia as its regional HQ in Latin America after considering LGBT+ and women's rights in several countries in the region. In particular, it compared legislation on sexual harassment and equal compensation, as well as maternity and paternity leave. Another area Kelly identifies is to 'help global teams understand locally driven diversity and inclusion priorities'. She comments that 'while discrimination (and the importance of combating it) is universal, we found that the specifics of the Black Lives Matter movement and systemic racism towards Black Americans were confusing to many of our employees outside of the United States'.

The concrete action was to include background information about the oppression of the Black community in the USA in connection with company-wide anti-racism training. Kelly added, 'While it might not be immediately obvious why an employee in Tokyo should learn about the history of slavery in the United States, if we want our global teams to work together, they need to understand one another's realities.' Although each local context is unique, there are often parallels that can be drawn from the situation in other places.

Exercise 3.1

Think about how diverse the organization you work for is and how you can contribute to making it more inclusive.

Going further

Catalyst (2014) *Diversity Matters*, New York: Catalyst, available at www.catalyst.org/research/infographic-diversity-matters/

Includes useful summaries of research findings and the business case for diversity, with a focus on gender diversity.

Centre for Global Inclusion: https://centreforglobalinclusion.org/

A non-profit organization which helps organizations manage diversity and foster inclusion.

Charta der Vielfalt [Diversity Charter]: www.charta-der-vielfalt.de/en/understanding-diversity/diversity-management/

German diversity network with useful materials in German and English.

Johansson, F. (2004) *The Medici Effect: What Elephants and Epidemics Can Teach Us about Innovation*, Boston, MA: Harvard Business Review Press.

An exploration of how diversity drives innovation.

4

Brains and Bells

Making Better Decisions

We don't see things as they are. We see them as we are.

Rabbi Shemuel ben Nachmani, Talmud

Key questions

- What is bias?
- How can we mitigate the negative effects of bias?

Thanks to the exciting developments in neuroscience, enabled by technological developments, new insights into the functioning of the brain are helping us to understand better how it works. Knowing this is a key part of making better decisions and creating more inclusive organizations. Before we look at this in more depth try a couple of quick awareness-raising exercises. Suggested answers can be found at the back of the book.

Perceptions

Tables

Exercise 4.1

Look at the two tables (Figure 4.1). Which one is longer? Which is wider?

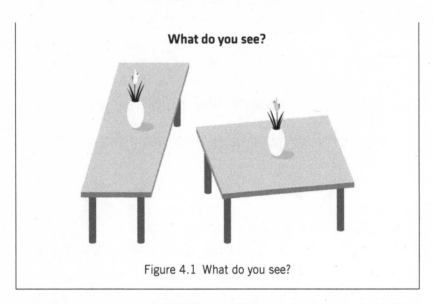

What do you see?

Figure 4.1 What do you see?

Car crash

Exercise 4.2

Explain what is happening here:

A father and his son were involved in a car crash, and the man died at the scene. When the child arrived at the hospital and was taken to the operating theatre, the surgeon stepped back and said: 'I can't operate on this boy. He's my son.'

People tend to imagine that the brain is purely rational and neutral, but in both these cases it seems to be misleading us in some way. Research shows how this works. A good starting point is to look at how we make judgements, and an interesting starting point is how we decide that something tastes good.

Wine tasting

The University of Bonn (2017) carried out an experiment based on wine tasting. Test persons were placed in a magnetic resonance imaging (MRI) scanner which recorded the activity of their brains during the tasting. They were shown the price before tasting and then after tasting it they were asked to rate the wine. The researchers used a wine costing €12, but the price was randomly shown to the test persons as €3, €6 and €18. As expected, the subjects ranked the wine with the higher price more positively than the apparently cheaper one.

The MRI scanner results confirmed this. 'The research team discovered that above all parts of the medial pre-frontal cortex and also the ventral striatum were activated more when prices were higher. While the medial pre-frontal cortex particularly appears to be involved in integrating the price comparison and thus the expectation into the evaluation of the wine, the ventral striatum forms part of the brain's reward and motivation system. The reward and motivation system is activated more significantly with higher prices and apparently increases the taste experience in this way.'

Bias, prejudice and discrimination

One aspect of the brain 'misleading' us is bias. The word 'bias' (from the French for 'oblique') is thought to have entered the English language through the game of bowls, where it referred to balls which was heavier on one side. Applied to the mind, it means that there is an unfair weight in favour of or against someone or something. Bias can be negative or positive, conscious or unconscious. Prejudice is a biased opinion which is not based on reason or experience. Most people, while admitting that they have prejudices, assume that they are less prejudiced than others. Prejudice can lead to discrimination, which is the unjust treatment of different categories of people.

Unconscious bias

Unconscious bias is a major barrier to inclusion and good decision-making. Its effects can be seen in many different areas. They are particularly obvious in the recruiting process. You want to hire the best person for the job, but even before you invite candidates to an interview biases start to get in the way. You are inevitably influenced by photographs, names or other parts of the application which do not have a direct bearing on the job.

Adesina and Marocico (2017), journalists from the BBC, sent CVs from two candidates who had identical skills and experience in response to a hundred job advertisements in London. One candidate was called Adam Henton and the other Mohamed Allam. Adam Henton was offered three times more interviews than Mohamed Allam. Researchers were shocked to find this discrimination against someone with a Muslim-sounding name in one of the world's most multicultural cities. This has serious implications when you consider that recruiters decide whether to look more carefully at a CV after, on average, just 5–7 seconds. First impressions really do count.

Racial bias can be found in biometric technology for facial or voice recognition. Young (2020) reports on research which shows how the rate of inaccuracy for identifying Asian and African American faces was ten to a hundred times higher than that for images of Caucasians. The bias comes from the data at the basis of the system; these problems will continue to occur if different types of people are not included in the design.

These sorts of bias are related to the dimensions in the Wheel of Difference (see Chapter 3). Think about biases in your business. Are men hired rather than women for top management positions? Do you hire employees over 50? Are you open to people with a different ethnic or racial background from yourself and the majority of your colleagues? Are you reluctant to promote single parents or women with small children? Do you have a preference for graduates from particular universities? How accepted are members of the LGBT+ community? Are extroverts more likely to be promoted than introverts? Would you have hired Stephen Hawking?

The defensive brain

To understand why we have biases it helps to look more closely at mental shortcuts. The average adult brain makes up only about 2 per cent of our body mass, but it consumes about 20 per cent of our energy. As a result, it has evolved to make mental shortcuts to save energy. We cannot cope with all the information that we are bombarded with; every second; we are exposed to 11 million bits of information but can process only about 40 bits. This means that we constantly filter information.

Humans are wired to make quick decisions to survive. If you see a lion in the jungle, you have to react. You don't have the time to check whether it is a friendly lion or not. Although this mechanism is vital for survival, it can also mislead us. You think you see a dangerous snake on the path in front of you and react immediately, only to find out that it is a harmless branch from a tree. The brain does not distinguish between physical and emotional safety. In intercultural encounters, we may feel misunderstood or find ourselves in stressful situations, and the brain may respond to this discomfort in the same way it would to a physical threat. We may be away from home, have jet lag, be confronted with a different language, are struggling to adapt to the climate and diet, and are under pressure to get quick results.

Casey and Robinson (2017) describe how this works. The oldest part of the brain from an evolutionary point of view is the 'reptilian', or lower, brain which is linked directly to our survival functions such as breathing, heartbeat, digestion and balance. The limbic system which developed later governs emotion and memory. The most recent part of the brain to develop is the cerebral cortex, which is the centre for thinking and consciousness. When there is a perceived threat, the brain goes into defence mode and responds with fight, flight or freeze. 'It destabilizes the prefrontal cortex and takes the higher brain offline.' While these mechanisms make sense from an evolutionary point of view they don't always lead to good decision-making.

Kahneman (2011) talks about two ways of thinking, which he calls 'fast' and 'slow'. Fast or 'System One thinking ... operates automatically and quickly, with little or no effort and no sense of voluntary control.' Slow or 'System Two thinking allocates attention to the effortful mental activities that demand it, including complex computations. The operations of System Two are often associated with the subjective experience of agency, choice and concentration.'

Nguyen-Phuong-Mai (2020) points out how fear is culturally conditioned. 'There is a complex dialogue between the amygdala (emotional memory) and the hippocampus (factual memory) in the formation of fear.' If our memory is positive it will trigger reward pathways, but if it is negative it will trigger fear. 'We are shaped by what we remember.' Goleman (1995) talks about an 'amygdala hijack' when our emotional response is immediate, overwhelming and out of proportion to the actual stimulus.

Types of cognitive bias

Stereotyping

Stereotyping is assuming a person has characteristics because they are a member of a particular group; stereotypes are fixed ideas of what a particular type of person or thing is like. The word, which derives from the Greek word stereos for firm or solid, was originally used in the world of printing. Stereotypes were developed in the late eighteenth century to speed up the printing of newspapers with large print runs. They are made by locking columns of type and illustration plates into a matrix, which is then used to cast a stereotype plate from metal.

There is nothing new about stereotypes. In multicultural Austria in the eighteenth century innkeepers painted *Völkertafel*, or 'panels of peoples', on the walls of their taverns to help the increasing number of travellers in Central Europe orient themselves to the different sorts of people that they might encounter on their journeys. In London you can buy postcards depicting popular European stereotypes: 'cooking like a Brit', 'talkative as a Finn', 'driving like the French' and 'organized as a Greek'. It's appealing to be able to put groups into convenient categories: as George Clooney's character in the film *Up in the Air* famously says, 'I stereotype, it's fast.' Stereotypes can be entertaining if they are about another culture, but irritating if they are about your own.

Researchers have looked at how far there is any truth in these sorts of stereotypes. As Merali (2005) reports, research carried out at the US National Institutes of Health shows how there is little truth in this sort of national stereotyping. More than 40,000 adults from 49 cultures were surveyed. 'The researchers found that there was no correlation between perceived cultural characteristics and the actual traits rated for real people ... Stereotypes about national character seem to be largely cultural constructions, transmitted through the media, education, history, hearsay, and jokes.' Researcher Antonio Terracciano comments: 'People should trust less in their own beliefs about national character. These can be dangerous and the basis for discrimination.'

It is clear that stereotypes reflect the society in which we live. Hinton (2020) talks about stereotypes as 'culture in mind' and makes the case that stereotypes ought not to be 'demonized' as 'monsters in the mind'. 'Generalizations about people are learnt from the culture that the person inhabits. Socialization, in terms of formal and informal education, means that people acquire these associations to become cultural beings, able to interact with fellow cultural group members in communication.'

Maybe it is more helpful to talk about 'cultural filters' or 'cultural lenses' through which we see the world. We need to categorize knowledge in order to make sense of it, and our images of particular groups of people are built up over many years from the input that we have been exposed to in society, at home, school, work and through the media. The algorithms at the heart of social media identify these filters and, through the selection of what we see, have the effect of reinforcing them. The problem with these cultural filters is that they blind us to the real qualities of individuals and can lead us to make inaccurate, misleading and unhelpful assessments of people.

There are many other types of cognitive bias. Some of the most important ones for business people are listed here:

- **Similarity bias** happens when we like people who are similar to us, as opposed to people who appear different: 'She went to the same university as I did; she must be good.' When people talk about 'the right chemistry' or 'culture fit', they are often simply looking for a 'mini me'.

- **Affective heuristic bias** is based on an emotional reaction. We make a quick decision based on an emotional reaction rather than looking at the evidence: 'I know my people. I just follow my gut feeling – that's why I'm so successful.'

- **Confirmation bias** selectively searches for information that confirms our previously existing beliefs: 'The Koreans I know are hard-working. I'm sure that the Korean who has applied for the job will be hard-working.'

- The **halo effect** is a bias in which our overall impression of a person affects our evaluations of that person's specific traits: 'He is such a good engineer. I'm sure he'll succeed as a manager.'

- The **horns effect** is the negative equivalent of the halo effect: 'I'll never forget what he said at the meeting last year – no way are we going to promote him.'

- **Groupthink** refers to when we are influenced by the opinions of others in a group: 'All the others think that she is the right candidate – I suppose they must be right.'

- **Anchoring bias** is based on the tendency to rely too heavily on the first piece of information offered when making decisions. We hear that 'he has an MBA from Harvard but can be quite aggressive' and focus on the MBA from Harvard rather than his potentially difficult personality.

Microaggressions

Microaggressions are minor actions which reveal an underlying bias. Here are some examples:

- who you sit next to on a bus or train
- who you include or ignore at a meeting
- making no attempt to pronounce a foreign name correctly
- imitating someone's accent when they speak a language other than their own
- rolling your eyes when talking to someone
- 'mansplaining': when a man explains something in a condescending way to a woman who knows more about it than him
- asking someone: 'Where are you from?'

The last example might seem like an innocent question and it can be, but it can also indicate that you think the other person doesn't belong. If someone has always lived in a society or tried hard for many years to integrate, then it is frustrating for them to keep having to explain their origins, just because they look different or speak with an accent.

Black people born in predominantly white societies complain of constantly being asked where they are from. When they answer they may well be asked, 'But where are you really from?' Taiye Selasi, a writer and photographer of Nigerian and Ghanaian descent, who was born in London and raised in Boston, Massachusetts, and lives in Rome and Berlin, talks about her reaction to this question in her 2014 TED Talk 'Don't ask me where I'm from, ask where I'm local' (Selasi, 2014). More serious forms of discrimination include being asked to show your ID or being stopped and searched by the police just because of your appearance.

Addressing bias

We are all biased in some way; we all have our own cultural filters. We can, to some extent, become aware of them but we cannot get rid of, train away or 'cure' unconscious bias. Having accepted that, it is important to reduce the potentially negative effects and go from unconscious bias to conscious inclusion. This needs to be done at individual, team and organizational levels.

Individual level

Take the Implicit Association Test (IAT)

The implicit-association test (IAT) was produced by Project Implicit at Harvard University. It assesses users' preferences on more than 90 different topics ranging from pets to political issues, ethnic groups to sports teams, and entertainers to styles of music. Banaji and Greenwald (2013) describe how the test aims to reveal the 'hidden biases of good people'. An increasing number of critics like Hinton (2020) have questioned the scientific validity and usefulness of the IAT. It is sometimes used as the basis for a quick-fix anti-discrimination training which has been shown to have little or no impact. It does, however, remain one of the most widely used tools in the field and can be a useful starting point for reflection and discussion. It should, however, not be used in isolation but must be part of a wider package of measures.

Use the circle of trust

This is a quick exercise you can do by yourself or with team members:

List five people, excluding family members, who you trust most.

Using the Wheel of Difference (see Chapter 3) reflect on how many of the diversity dimensions are included in the people on your list. Compare your results with those of your colleagues.

Watch your language

Make sure you use inclusive or non-derogatory language. This means, for instance using 'they' instead of 'he' or 'she'. Avoid generalizations such as comments that begin 'That type of person ...' Use 'work days' instead of 'man days' and 'blocking list' instead of 'blacklist'. If you translate into other languages, check that the translation is also inclusive – inclusion gets easily get lost in translation.

'Flip it to test it'

Milne (2018) describes how Kristen Pressner developed this idea while she was Global Head of HR for Roche Diagnostics. She realized that she had been treating similar pay requests made by male and female team members differently, reacting less favourably to the female leaders. She then started to use the 'flip it to test it' approach on herself. It involves swapping the gender of the person in any situation and seeing how it feels. An example is to feel the difference between someone saying, 'He is a strong and assertive leader' and, 'She is a strong and assertive leader'.

Connect with diverse stakeholders

To try to change your attitude to groups that you suspect you are biased about, find out more about them. One simple way of doing this is to spend more time with people who are different from yourself. Go for a drink or lunch with someone you instinctively have negative feelings about and try to get to know them. It's sometimes surprising how we can change our view of people when we get to know them better. On social media deliberately connect with and follow people who have different views from you or who you don't immediately find attractive – this will radically change what appears on your feed.

Become an ally

You can't change an organization by yourself – to do this you need allies. Melaku et al. (2020) describe how people in positions of power can become allies to marginalized colleagues. They call allyship 'a strategic mechanism used by individuals to become collaborators, accomplices and co-conspirators who fight injustice and promote equity in the workplace through supportive personal relationships and public acts of sponsorship and advocacy'. They suggest a number of practical ways of doing this which include educating yourself, recognizing your privilege, accepting feedback, being available as a confidant, 'bringing diversity to the table', speaking out if you witness discrimination, sponsoring marginalized co-workers, insisting on diverse candidates when hiring and 'building a community of allies'.

Team level

Ring the bell

As for bias at the team level, you can start to address it by challenging bias in team meetings. Speak up when someone says something that you feel is biased. One way of doing this is to have a hotel reception bell on the table and encourage colleagues to ring it and stop the meeting if they hear biased comments. This can be done in virtual meetings by agreeing on an icon, like a raised hand, which indicates that you want to report a bias. If you do this in every meeting it can become tiresome, but do it now and again to make the point.

Share unconscious bias moments

Have an 'unconscious bias moment' at the beginning of important decision-making meetings to remind the team of key aspects of unconscious bias. Get team members to make short selfie videos about their own unconscious bias moments and share them. Make sure that the team leader and management set an example and also share their bias moments.

Organizational level

Use nudging techniques

Thaler and Sunstein (2009) describe how 'nudging' can be used to improve decisions about 'health, wealth and happiness'. Kepinski and

Nielsen (2020) define a nudge as a 'relatively weak and non-intrusive mental push that will help the brain to make better decisions'.

A famous example of this was when nudging was used to help solve a problem at Amsterdam airport. The airport authorities found that they were spending an excessive amount of money on cleaning the men's toilets. They tried to deal with this by putting up signs in different languages, asking the users to be more careful. This had little effect. What did work was to add small targets to the urinals. The idea was to challenge the men to be more accurate. This idea is now widely used in men's toilets with many types of target including golf holes and football goals. Other examples of nudges are to place healthy food options at eye level in a canteen while putting junk food in places that are harder to reach.

Review recruiting and development processes

A famous example of this concerns orchestras in the USA which found that they were not hiring many women musicians. The numbers increased radically when they introduced 'blind auditions' with the musicians playing behind a screen so that they couldn't be seen by the selection panel.

Have processes in place to make sure that the recruiting and development of employees is as fair as possible. This can include removing photographs, names and gender from CVs, as well as looking critically at the channels you use for recruitment. Are you focusing too much on a few limited sources? How diverse are the potential candidates from these sources? If you want to hire diverse candidates, make sure that this diversity is reflected in the selection panels.

Don't stop at recruiting. Bias can negatively influence the development of employees. Sometimes we put people into mental boxes such as 'He's always a high performer' or 'She never says anything in meetings' and this can colour our judgement in discussions about which employees should be considered for promotion. That's why it is important to try to 'unbox' individuals in performance reviews by questioning exactly why someone should be promoted or not. Make sure the criteria that are used are clear and transparent and that you apply them rigorously; it's striking how often people make up or change their criteria to fit the candidate that they have chosen.

Publicize positive role models

Run a media campaign with positive role models. The most powerful way is to find examples from within the company, but you can also include role models from the outside world. An example would be the Welsh all-round talent Tanni Grey-Thompson who was born with spina bifida and is a wheelchair user but has had a successful career as a Paralympic athlete, in politics and as a TV presenter. She has provided inspiration for many people with similar conditions.

Provide mentorship

Make sure that mentorship programmes are open to all different groups of employees and deliberately connect employees who have different backgrounds. This could include a senior colleague mentoring someone who has just joined the company or people from different departments mentoring each other.

Offer effective training

Many companies run training programmes connected with unconscious bias and diversity. For these to be effective it is important that training is not treated as an isolated solution. Be suspicious of training providers who promise to 'reboot your brain' or 'banish unconscious bias' with a short one-time intervention. You can't go to the gym once and then be fit enough to run a marathon.

Some companies make diversity training mandatory for all employees. While this might seem like a good way of showing that they are taking discrimination seriously, it is unlikely that compulsory training will be effective and, at worst, can be counterproductive and lead to a negative backlash.

Good training is based on authentic material and interaction. Collect real cases of bias and discrimination from colleagues in focus groups and use them as a basis for discussion. Make sure that at the end of the training participants commit to concrete actions and that there is follow-up.

Use Artificial Intelligence (AI)

It is tempting to think that AI will remove bias. It can never be completely neutral as it, too, is inevitably influenced by the people who produce the algorithms and the environment in which they are working.

Make a personal plan

Exercise 4.3

Think about how you can mitigate the negative effects of unconscious bias in your sphere of influence. Discuss your ideas with your team. Make sure that everyone records their commitment to change and fix a time to review the commitments.

Commitment card

Use a card like the one shown in Figure 4.2 to record your commitments to mitigating bias. Make sure that you review the commitments regularly, by yourself or with other members of your team.

Area of responsibility	Potential for more diversity	Actions
1. Learning and development	80% of external trainers over age of 40.	Increase number of younger trainers by 20% over two years.
2. Coordination of training in APAC region	No local trainers.	Hire a local coordinator in APAC region in six months.

Figure 4.2 Commitment card

Scientific work on how the brain functions can be used to appeal to people who have previously been sceptical about diversity issues. People who may be reluctant to accept the soft arguments may be more likely to be convinced by the hard scientific data. Talking about how the brain works can help take the heat out of this highly charged topic and increase the sense of urgency in addressing cognitive biases so that you can improve decision-making and create a more inclusive organization.

Going further

Implicit Association Test. Free online unconscious bias test: https://implicit.harvard.edu/implicit/research/

Kahneman, D. (2011) *Thinking, Fast and Slow*, London: Penguin.
The classic introduction to how the brain makes judgements and decisions.

Kepinski, L. and Nielsen, T.C. (2020) *Inclusion Nudges Guidebook*, 3rd edn, Independently published.
A collection of practical ways of reducing the influence of cognitive bias.

Nguyen-Phuong-Mai, M. (2020) *Cross-Cultural Management: With Insights from Brain Science*, New York: Routledge.
A thoroughly researched overview of insights from neuroscience and how they relate to intercultural management.

Shaules, J. (2015) *The Intercultural Mind: Connecting Culture, Cognition and Global Living*, Boston, MA: Intercultural Press.
An introduction to the influence of culture on the unconscious mind.

5

The Intercultural Cocktail

Navigating Cultures

You can make fish soup from a fish, but not fish from a fish soup.

Chinese proverb

Key questions
- What are the most important cultural influencing factors?
- How can we talk about cultural differences without stereotyping?

When faced with the complexity of intercultural interactions, it is tempting to look for easy solutions. Downloading lists of dos and don'ts about a specific culture before going on a business trip will provide you with some basic information, but the tips on behaviour can be misleading. How we behave doesn't just depend on culture but on a number of interconnected factors. Culture is like salt in the soup – you can taste it but you can't separate it from the rest of the soup.

The danger is to rely on advice which is based on generalizations about a national culture – however true they are, they will probably not apply to the specific individuals that you are dealing with. This chapter looks at how to understand the influence of cultural factors without resorting to misleading stereotypes.

The intercultural cocktail

The three-factor model developed by Barmeyer and Haupt (2007) is a useful starting point for a deeper understanding of this complexity. To understand what is happening in any given situation, you need to consider not just culture but the interplay between the individual, culture in all its forms and the context in which you are working. This is shown in Figure 5.1, showing the 'intercultural cocktail'.

Intercultural Cocktail

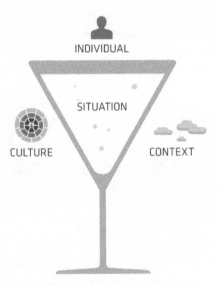

Figure 5.1 The intercultural cocktail

- **Individual.** We do some things, like eating and breathing, because we are human beings, some things because we are a member of a group and some things because of our individual personality. A key to understanding what is happening in any situation is to start with the individual and their uniqueness.

- **Context.** Context plays a vital role in determining what happens in any situation. What is happening in the wider environment in which you are working? This can include the political and economic situation, the market as well as the size and type of project. Are you in a boom or a recession? Is it a buyers' or sellers' market?

- **Culture.** Relevant cultural factors can be found in the Wheel of Difference (see Chapter 3). You will not need to consider all of these types of difference to understand every situation. The key is to identify the ones which are likely to have the most impact.

Research into cultural dimensions

Just as there are many different types of culture, so culture itself is multidimensional. Defining cultural dimensions has been a primary focus of attention for interculturalists in the second half of the twentieth century. Although most of the research has been on national cultures, the dimensions that have been developed can usefully be applied to many different types of culture.

Early ideas came from the USA where people were faced with the challenge of finding ways of helping people from many different cultural origins to live and work together. There was an increased realization after the Second World War that it was necessary to know more about other cultures in order to work successfully abroad. Input came from the military, businesses and the Peace Corps, which were all faced with the challenges of operating in many different and unfamiliar places.

Some of the first research was done by Edward T. Hall, an anthropologist who worked at the US Foreign Service Institute training government employees in the 1950s. He became famous for his work on communication and different concepts of time. Geert Hofstede, a social psychologist and engineer from the Netherlands, was the first to carry out large-scale quantitative research in the intercultural field. He collected data from employees of IBM in the late 1960s and early 1970s. His database covered employees in 72 national subsidiaries, 38 occupations and 20 languages. There were more than 116,000 questionnaires, each with over a hundred questions. He published his findings in 1980 in a ground-breaking book called *Culture's Consequences*, which has had an enormous influence on the further development of the field. He initially identified four dimensions – individualism/collectivism; uncertainty avoidance; power distance; and masculinity/femininity – later adding long-term orientation and indulgence/restraint. A summary of his results can be found in Hofstede et al. (2010). Trompenaars and Hampden-Turner (2020) continued this work, adding further dimensions of their own.

The Global Leadership and Organizational Behavior Effectiveness (GLOBE) research project has built on Hofstede's work. Starting in the 1990s it has become one of the largest and most comprehensive studies of its kind and has a global research team. A summary of the results can be found in House (2004). Globe 2020 examines cultural practices, leadership ideals and trust in more than 160 countries, involving over 500 researchers. The World Values Survey (WVS) is an international research programme devoted to the study of social, political, economic, religious and cultural values of people in the world. It operates in more than 120 world societies and carries out a global survey every five years.

The German interculturalist Alexander Thomas has developed a method defining 'culture standards' based on analysis of people's reactions to critical incidents. Thomas et al. (2010) apply the approach to specific national cultures. Other popular models based on cultural dimensions have been developed by Lewis (2018) and Meyer (2015).

Work on cultural dimensions from the USA and the Netherlands has, until recently, dominated the intercultural field, but there is now an increasing realization of the need for perspectives from researchers with more diverse backgrounds. Deardorff (2009) tries to compensate for the western Anglo-Saxon bias of the literature by including approaches from other countries in her handbook on intercultural competence.

Nwosu (2009) describes the need for models suitable for use by the 3,000 ethnic groups with 1,000 languages in 54 countries on the African continent. He identifies five important dimensions which he considers to be especially important in this context:

'approach to self and other, approach to social relations, approach to time, approach to work and communication forms and styles'.

Manian and Naidu (2009) stress the concept of 'oneness' in India: 'India's contribution to intercultural competence is in the core principle of 'oneness' of recognizing differences while focusing on commonality.' Moosmüller and Schönhuth (2009) point out that there is 'a challenge for theorists and researchers to criticize and deconstruct the old concepts of intercultural competence and to intensify efforts to construct and refine new concepts'.

Navigating cultures

The Culture Navigation System (Figure 5.2) is a practical tool to help you understand critical situations in international business. The intention is not to provide a comprehensive list or a static map of cultures but rather a selection of the most important cultural factors that can influence situations in different contexts.

Culture Navigation System

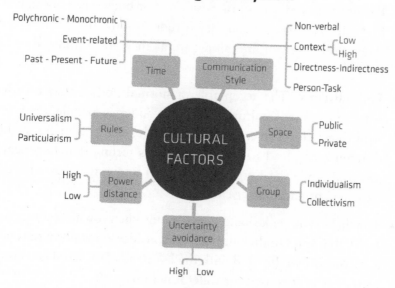

Figure 5.2 Culture Navigation System

Communication style

Non-verbal communication

Even before you speak, your appearance, gestures and body language are sending messages to the people around you. Estimates vary but it seems that 70–90 per cent of our communication is non-verbal, and so it is important to be aware of the non-verbal cues you are sending.

- **Gestures** which have a positive meaning in one culture can be negative or even offensive in another. While in Britain and Australia the two-finger V-sign is a rude gesture when the palm of the hand faces inwards, in many other cultures it is understood as 'two' or 'victory'. In China people count from one to ten with one hand; if you make a fist and extend your thumb upwards and first finger forward this means eight, not two as non-Chinese might think. Be careful in a bar in Shanghai when ordering drinks, because if you get it wrong you will end up with eight beers instead of two!

- **Posture.** The way you sit or position your body sends out signals. In Arab countries it is considered rude to show the soles of your shoes to people you are talking to, as they are considered to be dirty.

- **Body distance.** The acceptable or normal body distance varies between different cultures. In Latin America people generally tend to get closer to each other than Northern Europeans. This difference can lead to Latin Americans feeling that Europeans are cold while the Europeans can feel uncomfortable with the closeness of Latin Americans.

- **Touch.** Do you shake hands, kiss or hug when you meet someone? In Islamic and Hindu cultures it is considered insulting to touch someone or handle food with the left hand. This hand is considered dirty as it is used for toilet functions.

- **Facial expressions.** In some cultures it is considered strange to smile at everybody; smiling requires a particular reason to smile. A US fast-food chain was pleased with the sales figures in its new restaurant in Moscow, but on a site visit to check quality standards the US regional manager was shocked at what they felt was the unfriendliness of the local staff. 'They don't even smile when serving customers,' they commented and recommended that the local staff should go on a customer orientation course. While for this US manager smiling is considered to be a sign of friendliness, for the Russian staff smiling without a reason is taken to indicate superficiality or even stupidity. There is a Russian saying that 'the one who smiles without reason, has nothing in their head'.

- **Eye contact** differs across cultures. The question is whether you make eye contact at all and, if you do, how intense it is. In some Arab cultures it is inappropriate for a man to make eye contact with a woman. In some cultures, it is considered to be a sign of respect not to look your superior in the eye in a conflict situation.

- **Paralanguage.** This concerns the tone, pitch and intonation of speech. Giggling may be a sign not of a humorous situation but of embarrassment. In some cultures, it is considered a sign that you are enjoying the food if you slurp your soup or belch. What volume is acceptable varies widely.

- **Turn-taking.** This is about how we structure a discourse and the role of silence in conversations.

- **Smell.** Attitudes to, and tolerance of, different smells vary in different cultures. While some cultures require body odours to be covered with cosmetics, others consider body odours to be natural and pleasing. This can cause tension when people from different cultures share office space.

- **Clothing.** There are no universal rules on what is appropriate to wear for business in different cultural settings. Even the interpretation of 'business casual' varies widely depending on where you are.

Context

Do you make your message explicit or do you expect people to 'read between the lines'? Nisbett (2003) reports on an experiment in which students at Kyoto University and the University of Michigan were shown pictures of an underwater scene. Of course, there were individual differences, but the Japanese students tended to comment more on the background elements, such as rocks, bubbles and plants, as well as the relationships between the objects. The first thing that most of the Japanese commented on was the environment, whereas the Americans referred to the fish before anything else.

In another experiment he showed students from China and the USA sets of words like panda, monkey and banana and asked them which two words belonged together. The US participants tended to connect the panda and the monkey: they categorized the items. The Chinese linked the monkey with the banana; they preferred to think in terms of relationships.

Hall (1976) developed the idea of low- and high-context cultures which can be helpful in understanding such fundamentally different ways of thinking. In *low-context* cultures the message is made explicit, whereas in *high-context* cultures you have to take into account the context. The Japanese talk about 'reading the air'. In high-context cultures the conversation may start with general topics and take some time to 'get to the point' whereas in low-context cultures people will start with specific information and then go to the general point. In low-context cultures written documents will contain more detail, so an agenda or CV will be longer than in a high-context culture. A report may contain more references and guidelines.

A further example of high-context culture is in rural communities where there is a high level of shared common knowledge. For example, a bus stop may not even be marked; everyone knows that the bus stops at the large tree in the village square. In industrialized societies the stop will be clearly marked and on it there will be a timetable and details of how to buy a ticket – little common shared knowledge is assumed. This is an example of a low-context culture.

Directness or indirectness

Is direct communication valued or not? British English is full of polite phrases such as 'I'm afraid I can't come today', 'Would you mind opening the window?' or 'I was wondering if ...' These can easily confuse people from more direct cultures who think: 'Why are they afraid? Why don't they just say, "Open the window."' They may wonder: 'What do they really want?' For some directness can be equated with honesty and transparency, while for others it is considered to be impolite. As the saying goes: 'The Germans are too honest to be polite whereas the British are too polite to be honest.'

British understatement or self-deprecation can puzzle people from cultures where communication is direct. 'If he's really a world expert why does he say: "I don't know why you invited me today, I'm only just beginning to understand this topic."' It seems more like a bizarre admission of incompetence than a modest assertion of his credentials.

Person/task

Is it more important to build up a relationship before working together or to get down to the task as quickly as possible? Any interaction involves relationships and actions, but cultures differ as to how important these are and what is done first. In some cultures, it will be essential to get to know your business partner personally before starting to do business. In more task-based cultures people will focus on getting the task done first; if that is successful, they may socialize with their business partners afterwards.

Space

Is there a clear division between work and pleasure? How far do you socialize with colleagues and customers? This is not just about physical space but how we see our public and private sphere. The model of the peach and coconut shows two different approaches

(Figure 5.3). The peach has a soft exterior that indicates friendliness and a large public sphere. If you see a stranger in the lift in a hotel, you will greet them. The coconut, on the other hand, has a hard exterior which indicates a large private sphere, which is hard to access. For the coconut it seems strange to greet people who you don't know. Confusion can result when the two types overlap. When the coconut is greeted by first names or invited to the home of the peach they may interpret this as a sign of close friendship. For the peach these acts don't indicate anything special, but the coconut may be disappointed when the relationship doesn't develop.

Peaches and coconuts can attribute the behaviour of the other in negative and positive ways. The coconut sees the peach as superficial, and the peach sees the coconut as unfriendly. In a positive way the coconut can see the peach as open and flexible, and the peach can see the coconut as trustworthy and reliable.

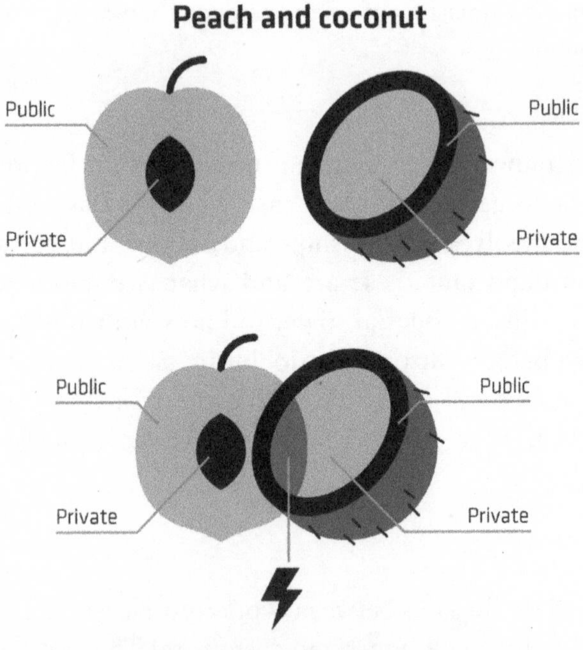

Peach and coconut

Public

Private

Public

Private

Public

Private

Public

Private

Figure 5.3 The peach and the coconut
Adapted from Zaninelli, S. (1994) Vier Schritte eines integrativen Trainingsansatzes am Beispiel eines interkulturellen Trainings: Deutschland – USA, in *Materialien zum internationalen Kulturaustausch*, 33, Stuttgart: Institut für Auslandsbeziehungen. pp 5–8.

Group

Do you tend to make decisions individually or as a group? Hofstede et al. (2010) define individualism as where 'the ties between individuals are loose; everyone is expected to look after him – or herself and his or her immediate family'. The 'I' is more important than the 'we'. Collectivism is where people are 'integrated into strong, cohesive in-groups, which throughout people's lifetime continue to protect them in exchange for unquestioning loyalty'.

An example of collectivism can be found in the Zulu and Xhosa languages in South Africa where the word *ubuntu* is shorthand for a phrase meaning 'I am because we are' – the individual is defined by the group. In China, which is generally considered to have a high level of collectivism, a tangible sign of this is that in most restaurants people eat in groups and share food; tourist hotels often cater for large family groups with adjoining suites of rooms. In Colombia there is a saying: 'If you eat alone, you die alone.'

Uncertainty avoidance

Do you see the unknown as welcome or as a threat? Hofstede et al. (2010) define uncertainty avoidance as 'the extent to which the members of a culture feel threatened by ambiguous or unknown situations'. High uncertainty avoidance indicates a low tolerance for uncertainty and ambiguity, reflected in rule-orientation and controls to reduce uncertainty. Low uncertainty avoidance indicates less concern about uncertainty and ambiguity, reflected in less rule-orientation, acceptance of change, and more willingness to take risks. Countries with high uncertainty avoidance will have strict regulations on data protection.

Power distance

How steep is the hierarchy? According to Hofstede et al. (2010) power distance is 'the extent to which the less powerful members of institutions and organizations within a country expect and accept that power is distributed unequally'. In some cultures there is a large distance between the lowest person and the highest person in the hierarchy. In high power distance cultures leadership is centralized and status given to managers; there is a 'chain of command'. In lower power distance cultures power is distributed; the manager acts as one of the team and the organization held together by shared goals rather than strict hierarchical control.

Rules

Are rules universally binding or does their application depend on the situation and your relationship to those involved? Trompenaars and Hampden-Turner (2020) distinguish between universalist and particularist cultures. A classic example of this is whether or not you cross the road when the pedestrian light is red. In universalist cultures you will wait even if there is no traffic; a rule is a rule is a rule. In particularist cultures whether you cross or not will depend on the situation: you might generally follow the rule but make an exception if there is no traffic, if you are in a hurry or it is an emergency.

Time

- **Polychronic/monochronic.** Do you do several things at the same time or one thing at a time? In polychronic cultures it is normal to multitask; plans evolve and the agenda is open. In mono-chronic cultures it is normal to do one thing at a time, with fixed plans and agendas which are adhered to; time is seen as a limited resource which can be used, spent and wasted.

- **Event-related.** Do you follow a clear plan or do you do things as a result of what is going on around you? In an event-related culture the bus doesn't leave according to a timetable but when it is full. This is often associated with agricultural societies – you harvest the crops not according to a calendar but when the weather is right; time is not seen as a finite resource but part of the infinite cycles of the seasons.

- **Past, present and future.** Do you tend to focus on past achievements, the present or future benefits? Past-oriented cultures stress what has been done in the past, while future-oriented cultures stress the future. Depending on the development of a society people will have different ideas of what constitutes a 'long time'. In the USA, a relatively young country, 100 years is a long time.

Critical incidents

The critical incidents in this section illustrate the cultural factors in the Culture Navigation System (see above). Think about what is happening in the situations and which cultural factors might be playing a role. These are authentic cases; nationalities and countries have been removed so that you are not influenced by possible stereotypes. Suggested answers and the original countries can be found at the back of the book.

Critical incident: Missing the flight

Exercise 5.1

We missed the flight connection and were queuing at the airline counter to get new tickets. The customer in front of me from country A was complaining that no one had apologized for the delay; they threatened never to fly with the airline again. From where I was standing, I could see that the airline official from country B was tapping in data and concentrating hard on the computer display; within a few seconds they had handed the customer the new ticket. The customer walked away with a new flight but still complaining about the 'terrible service'.

Critical incident: Phones in meetings

Exercise 5.2

Several members of an international team are becoming increasingly concerned about the lack of discipline in team meetings. Some colleagues are constantly looking at their phones rather than taking part in the discussions; others see an important message and leave the room to make a call. This all makes it very hard to have a focused discussion on topics which require everyone's undivided attention. Some members of the team think that this behaviour is quite acceptable. The dissatisfied team members turn to the team leader for help.

Critical incident: How many parts?

Exercise 5.3

A binational team from countries A and B is working on a joint development project in the aerospace industry. At a meeting they agree that there should be three components in one of the modules; the decision is recorded in minutes. Two months later the colleagues from country B discover, by chance, that the team from country A is working on a prototype with only two components. When challenged, the team from country A say: 'But this is better and more cost-effective. What's the problem?' The team members from country B are annoyed.

Critical incident: Congratulations

Exercise 5.4

A manager from country A is working in country B. They are particularly impressed by the outstanding performance of one of the team. At the next *jour fixe* the manager praises this person in front of the group. The rest of the team members, who are all from country B, look uneasy.

Critical incident: The retreat

Exercise 5.5

The purpose-built management retreat has just opened in a beautiful location in the mountains in country A. No expense has been spared, with a top designer having been hired to create a clean, fresh space for informal top-level meetings. Managers and customers are encouraged to enjoy casual encounters in workshops, over a good meal and at the bar. To stress the 'no ranks, no titles' approach the bedrooms are all the same size with high-quality minimalist furnishings. 'Only waiters and bodyguards wear ties here,' commented one of the staff.

When the delegation of key customers from country B arrives their head of protocol complains that the rooms are not suitable and demands that they move to more prestigious accommodation. The CEO from country A is tied up with other meetings but is concerned about the reaction of the visitors and to improve the atmosphere suggests that the management team take the visitors out to dinner at a nearby restaurant, famous for its regional cuisine. The local management team eagerly await the evening meal and wait in the lobby for the transfer to the restaurant. The visitors come down the stairs, take one look at the group and get into the limousines without them. One of the drivers calls the organizer from country A and asks what they should do.

Critical incident: Slot reservation

Exercise 5.6

The customer in the oil industry in country A is impressed by the technology and expert knowledge provided by the sales managers from country B and is even prepared to accept the relatively high price in order to secure the quality needed for the prestigious project. As there is a high demand for the specialist product, the company from B demand a slot reservation fee from the customer in country A. This secures them a place on the waiting list, but this has to be renewed every three months. As far as the sales team is concerned this isn't an issue as the customers know that they will get their money back when they confirm the final order.

After several renewal agreements have been signed, the key account manager from B is called in to meet the client, but is taken aback when they have 'the shortest customer meeting' of their life. The customer makes it clear that they do not want to see them or their company again.

Tendencies

These critical incidents are examples of what can happen in particular situations – they are not meant to suggest that things *always* happen like this. Culture is like a river. Although the river is different at its source from what it is when it goes out into the sea, and different at its banks from in the main stream, it still keeps its identity as a river. As Adler (2008) said: 'Culture is what most of the people do most of the time.'

It is possible to describe tendencies. Figure 5.4 shows how this works when comparing two cultures. People in cultures A and B were asked at what time they would arrive at a dinner party when invited for 7 p.m. A stereotype would be to say, 'The Bs are always late'. A more constructive approach would be to recognize that, although there are individual differences in arrival times, there is a clear tendency for those from culture A to arrive earlier than those from culture B.

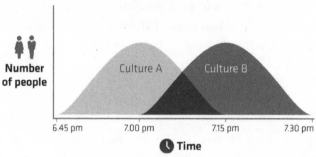

Figure 5.4 Tendencies

Of course, it is not just a matter of national cultural differences. What time people arrive will also depend on other factors: How old are the guests? Is it a formal dinner? How well do you know the host? Is it cold or hot outside? These can be more important than national cultural differences.

It is important not to assume that people from a particular country have the values typically found in that country. As Kirkman et al. (2016) point out: 'The biggest culture gaps are within countries, not between them ... An American walking down the street in Shanghai is likely to meet many Chinese people with values closer to his or her own than to an "average" Chinese.'

While cultural dimensions can be useful for understanding situations, it is important that they don't just become what Osland and Bird (2000) call 'sophisticated stereotypes'. The less we know about a culture the easier it is to be tempted to make generalizations. A danger is posed by the Dunning–Kruger effect, a type of cognitive bias in which people with little knowledge believe that they know more than they really do. In the intercultural setting this means people saying things like 'I worked there once for six months five years ago. I can tell you all about life there.'

The results of the research by Hofstede and others are snapshots taken of a group of people at a particular time, and, like a freeze frame in a film, they tell you about that moment but not about the whole plot. While they can be useful if you want to launch a marketing campaign or design the structure of an organization, they should not be used as a predictor of individual behaviour. In other words: 'You can make fish soup from a fish, but not fish from a fish soup.'

Going further

Furnham, A. and Petrova E. (2010) *Body Language in Business*, Houndmills: Palgrave Macmillan.
Authoritative guide to body language at work with examples from different cultures.
Hofstede, G., Hofstede G.J. and Minkov, M. (2010) *Cultures and Organisations: Software of the Mind. Intercultural Cooperation and Its Importance for Survival*, 3rd edn, New York: McGraw Hill.
The third edition of the book based on Hofstede's pioneering research. For the results of Geert Hofstede's research and country comparisons, see: www.hofstede-insights.com/product/compare-countries/
Nisbett, R.E. (2003) *The Geography of Thought: How Asians and Westerners Think Differently … and Why*, New York: Free Press.
A fascinating exploration of how people think differently in different cultures.
Trompenaars, F. and Hampden-Turner, C. (2020), *Riding the Waves of Culture: Understanding Diversity in Global Business*, 4th edn, London: Nicholas Brealey.
Classic guide to intercultural business based on the authors' 'seven dimensions'.

6

Decoding the Message

Intercultural Communication

The fool speaks, the wise man listens.

Ethiopian proverb

Key questions

- How can you communicate effectively with people from different cultures?
- How should you socialize with international business partners?

The way people communicate varies widely in different cultures. This chapter aims to provide you with some tools for finding the most effective communication style for different situations. The first exercise concerns a short, written message with more impact than you might expect.

Exercise 6.1

Look at the following message from a manager to an employee, Chris (Figure 6.1). Chris was annoyed and demotivated by the message. What do you think was happening?

Re: Cost optimization

Chris

The costs for travel expenses are much too high – let's discuss.

AB

Figure 6.1 Email

The 'Four sides of the message' model can be used to decode what is going on here.

Four sides of the message

Often people focus on the literal meaning of words used, but communication is more complicated than that. A useful model for decoding this complexity was developed by Schulz von Thun (1981) and is particularly suitable for application to intercultural communication. According to him, there are four sides to any message: content, appeal, self-disclosure and relationship.

Four sides of the message

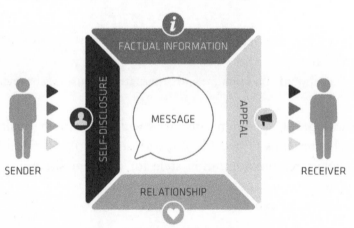

Figure 6.2 Four sides of a message

This can be used to analyse what is happening in Exercise 6.1. On the *content* level, the travel expenses are higher than planned – this is the fact behind the message. The *appeal* seems to be that the manager is asking Chris for a meeting or feedback. However, if the manager had really wanted to meet Chris, they would have sent an invitation for a specific time. Perhaps the appeal was more general and the manager was simply asking Chris to be more careful in the future.

The *self-disclosure* is that the manager reveals that they are under pressure to cut costs; maybe they are just passing on the pressure from their superior. The message also reveals something about their *relationship* with Chris: to interpret this properly more background information is required, but it could indicate that the manager doesn't trust Chris completely and feels that Chris doesn't have the costs under control. The fact that the manager addresses Chris by first name but signs the mail with their initials indicates an unequal or hierarchical relationship.

Chris was annoyed, not just because the manager is critical, but also because the criticism is not concrete. The manager could have attached a file with the data but instead left it vague so that it is unclear to Chris how serious the situation really is.

The manager needs to reflect on their communication style and think not just about their own situation but about the possible effects on the person receiving the message. It would help to provide more concrete information and, if things really are critical, arrange a time for a face-to-face meeting or, if this is not possible, at least a call.

Intercultural communication

Communication can be defined as the exchange of meaning. This involves the sending and receiving of information between a *sender* and a *receiver*. It happens not only through the use of words but also through non-verbal means, such as gestures and facial expression. The message received can be very different from the message sent.

A simplified model of communication goes as follows. An idea comes from the sender. This is encoded to produce a *message* which is transmitted through a *channel*. The channel is the medium used for communication (e.g. writing). The message is decoded by the receiver, who responds. The *context* is the environment in which the communication takes place. Noise is anything which distorts the message. Intercultural communication takes place when the sender and receiver are from different cultures. Communication can be challenging if the gap between the cultures is great; it can break down completely if there is too much *cultural noise*.

International netiquette

It is worth thinking about how culturally appropriate your text messaging and email communication is. Here are some general tips:

- Use emails for communicating information, not for criticism, sensitive or personal issues.

- KISS: Keep It Short and Simple. Unnecessarily long emails can create stress if you are writing to people in a foreign language. They will welcome shorter mails so that they don't have so much to read.

- Don't get emotional or 'flame'. Maybe you have misunderstood the message. Check by asking for clarification by giving the sender a quick call.

- Use the cc and bcc functions with care, especially when dealing with people from high power distance cultures; in extreme cases a critical email could lead to disciplinary action from the manager.

- Be sensitive as to how you address people. If they address you formally and use titles, then echo this when you reply to them.

- Be careful with emoticons. They look universal but aren't. Check the meaning in the target culture.

- Back up emails and text messages with face-to-face and phone communication.

- Use the language of your partner or international English.

Critical incident: Checking-in

Exercise 6.2

- What do you think is happening here?
- What cultural factors could be playing a role?

I am from country A and have to work a lot with country B these days. I thought my counterpart from B was really pleasant – they are always very friendly on the phone – until recently they let me down. A month earlier I had asked them to coordinate the collection of the quarterly sales figures from the sales team in our office in B. They said they would do it. When the deadline came they hadn't sent anything. When I called them to find out what had happened, they simply said, 'Oh yes, I'll do that as soon as I can, but it'll take a few days as we're really busy at the moment.' I was annoyed as they had promised to deliver on time.

A suggested answer can be found at the back of the book.

Presentations

Presentation styles differ in different cultures. Some presenters start with the main point and focus on practical examples with little or no theory; this is known as an *inductive* style and is popular in the UK and USA. Other presenters prefer the *deductive* style and explain the concept and methodology first before reaching a conclusion; this is popular in Germany. This difference in styles explains why many Germans find UK or US presentations superficial and Americans often find German presentations boring.

If your presentation is to be effective, try to find out what the preferred style of your audience is and adapt your approach accordingly. If you are speaking to a diverse audience with people from many different cultures, you will have to find a way to appeal to as many different types of people as possible, combining elements of different approaches.

Exercise 6.3

Imagine you are going to give an international business presentation. What do you think about the following techniques?

1. Starting with a joke
2. Reading a written text
3. Involving the audience
4. Keeping to the time limit
5. Making the structure very clear
6. Providing the audience with handouts
7. Dressing formally
8. Looking serious
9. Only taking questions at the end of the presentation
10. Using slides and other visual aids
11. Summarizing what you have said at the end of the presentation
12. Telling anecdotes

A suggested answer can be found at the back of the book.

Next time you are at an international meeting observe how people with different cultural backgrounds present. Think about how they deal with each of the techniques in the list.

Meetings

Businesspeople typically spend a large amount of time in meetings. Meetings with participants from different cultures can be challenging.

What do you think is happening in the following situations? What cultural factors could be playing a role? Suggested answers can be found at the back of the book.

Critical incident: Be prepared

Exercise 6.4

A manager from country A joins the management team of a company in country B. The weekly management meeting soon becomes a source of tension for both sides. The managers from B feel that their colleague from A is unprepared for the meetings as they turn up with a notepad and pen. The colleague from A wonders why they are having a meeting at all as the managers from B arrive with slides so full of detailed information that it seems that there is little left to discuss. Both sides are annoyed.

Critical incident: The budget meeting

Exercise 6.5

A and B are discussing the budget for development projects for the next business year. As usual things are tense as it's a question of how they are going to share the resources between the various departments. An observer notes that, as the conversation progresses, A stiffens and clenches their fist. B reacts by slumping back in their chair, opening up their arms and making jokes. A responds by stiffening even more and tapping on the table. When asked afterwards, B says that A is aggressive and A complains that B was not taking the discussion seriously.

Critical incident: Leadership training

Exercise 6.6

An IT team from country A is taking part in an international leadership training course. The instructors are from countries B and C and the course is held in English, although it has been agreed that the participants can speak their own language when doing the group work. When observing the group sessions one of the trainers comments: 'I don't understand what they're saying, but from the way they're talking it's clear they're having a major disagreement.' After the whole group comes back together the participants from A are surprised at the reaction of the trainer: they have in fact had a highly constructive conversation.

International meetings and events

Exercise 6.7

Look critically at the preparations and draft of an agenda for an international sales meeting in Figure 6.3. What improvements would you recommend to make the meeting as effective as possible? A suggested answer can be found at the back of the book.

Agenda: International Sales Meeting

Attendees: Sales representatives from Americas; Europe, Middle East and Africa (EMEA); Asia-Pacific (APAC).
Total number of participants: 57
Location: the production facility in UK

08.30   Opening speech (CEO)
09.00   Results: past financial year (CFO)
09.30   Presentations by regional sales heads
11.00   Q&A
11.30   Presentation by local plant manager
12.00   Lunch (finger food in conference room)
12.30   Factory tour
13.15   Presentations of new products:
  AX1, AX5B, KF53, KF88
15.15   Global sales process
17.00   Any other business
17.30   Closing speech (CEO)
18.30   Depart for dinner by shuttle bus
19.00   Dinner: Steak House, 10 Victoria Square
21.00   Return transfer from restaurant to hotel

Figure 6.3 Agenda

Checklist: International meetings and events

Here are some tips for running larger international meetings and events.

Are the aims of the meeting clearly defined?

Have you checked what the participants from different cultures expect from the meeting?

Is the location easily accessible for all participants?

Have you taken into consideration the language requirements of the participants?

Have you made allowance for the dietary requirements of the participants?

Do you have a local contact person responsible for the logistics?

Have you briefed the presenters and the chairperson or facilitator?

Does the agenda allow enough time for interaction?

Is the chairperson ready to take language and cultural differences into account?

Have you thought about appropriate follow-up after the meeting?

International business English

English has become established as a global standard language for business communication. This might seem to be good news for native speakers who will have an advantage. Of course, to some extent they do, but they also have to be careful.

Frequently non-native speakers of English complain that the native speakers are the ones who disrupt the communication in international meetings. The meeting is going well with everybody communicating happily in English as a second language until the colleagues from the USA and the UK turn up. According to Dignen and McMaster (2013) the following factors can cause irritation:

- speaking too fast
- speaking unclearly

- using unknown vocabulary

- using complicated sentence structure

- using idioms linked to their culture (e.g. from cricket or baseball)

- making jokes.

To ease the situation native speakers need to:

- slow down

- speak clearly

- restrict themselves to mainstream vocabulary (about 70 per cent of English can be generated with a vocabulary of 2,000 words)[1]

- use short and simple sentences, avoiding the passive forms of verbs

- avoid culturally linked idioms and references to sport and TV shows

- be careful to make sure that your humour is understandable for the people you are talking to. If in doubt, leave it out – and don't tell the great joke you have just heard and that you think is very funny; it is probably not a good export item.

Just as pilots use 'airspeak' – a globally standard restricted form of English international – so businesspeople need to master global business English. Speaking a foreign language can be exhausting, so make allowance for those whose English is not as good as yours. If during a meeting people start speaking with their colleagues in their own language, don't assume they are being rude or trying to hide something from you. They might just want to clarify something which they find difficult to do in English. Appreciate that it can be frustrating or even humiliating to have to work in a foreign

---

[1] A useful vocabulary list of common English words accessible to speakers of English as a foreign language is the 'Longman Defining Vocabulary' found in the *Longman Dictionary of Contemporary English*.

language. As one colleague said: 'When I speak English and they don't understand me I feel like a little child.' Understand that, if your colleagues sit in the bar after the meeting with colleagues from their own country, they are not necessarily being anti-social; they might just want a break from trying to talk English. To build lasting business relationships, native speakers of English should avoid the temptation of using language as a 'dirty trick', deliberately talking quickly or using obscure vocabulary and 'in-jokes'. Sometimes the best approach is to mix languages in a meeting. Show the slides in English with the speaker talking in the local language or vice versa. For important meetings when there is a more serious language gap consider employing a professional interpreter.

Using an interpreter

There are, of course, many parts of the world where English is not widely spoken and where it makes sense to use the services of an interpreter. As interpreters often have considerable international experience and an understanding of the mindsets of both sides they are predestined to act as bridge builders between cultures. They have considerable power as they can determine what is included, what is left out and how sensitive messages are conveyed.

Care should be taken in your choice of interpreter. In critical negotiations it is always advisable to have your own interpreter who you are sure will represent your interests. Ideally, you should have enough command of the language of your business partner to be able to get a feeling of the quality of the interpreting or translation provided. If not, and the content is important – for instance when drafting a contract – then find an independent translator to translate the text back into the original language (reverse translation).

Make sure your interpreter is properly briefed on the content so that they can familiarize themselves with any specialist terminology beforehand. Bear in mind that, if you are not using simultaneous interpreting, you will have to allow much more time for the meeting. Make sure that those speaking don't talk for a long period at a time but break up what they say into manageable chunks.

Socializing

Although relationships are at the core of any business, cultures vary as to how much time and effort are put into building them as opposed to doing tasks. In some cultures, getting to know a potential business partner is the basis of trust, while for people from task-based cultures this can be perceived as a 'waste of time'.

When German and British employees of the same company were asked how often they socialized with colleagues they answered the question very differently. The British said, 'Not very often', and when asked to clarify added: 'Only once a week when we go to the pub.' The Germans for their part said, 'Quite a lot', and when asked to clarify said: 'Three or four times a year: an annual team event, the Oktoberfest beer festival and the Christmas party.' This reflects a clear division between work and leisure by the Germans. There is even a saying in German: 'Dienst ist Dienst und Schnaps ist Schnaps' (literally: Work is work and liquor is liquor). For the British employees there is a more fluid relationship between public and private spheres and less separation of work and leisure.

Small talk

There is no universal answer to the frequently asked question as to which topics are suitable for small talk. The key is to develop a sense for topics that will build up a positive bond between you and avoid those that might offend the other person and create distance.

Look for signals that you can build on, for instance pictures or objects in the office or home. If you get a negative reaction to a topic then change the subject. If someone from the USA asks you how you are, then they probably don't really want to know all the details of your ailments but just expect a polite reply like, 'I'm fine, thank you' or, 'How are you?' In the UK talking about the weather is frequently used as a conversation opener – it is considered a good topic as the weather in Britain is changeable. This *phatic communication* has a social rather than an informative function. The message is not really about the weather but a signal that the communication channel is open.

Exercise 6.8

Before you read on, think about what small talk topics are acceptable in your culture (Figure 6.4).

Which topics would you talk about and to whom? Mark the ones you think would be appropriate with a plus sign (+) and those not advisable with a minus sign (–).

Topic	Person Colleague	Manager	Customer	Supplier	Friend	Partner	Parent
Weather							
Sport							
Family							
Politics							
Religion							
Salary							
Feelings							
Sex							
Illness							
Death							

Figure 6.4 Small talk

Which topics are taboo depends on the relationship you have with that person and the situation. You will talk about some things with family and friends that you would never dream about discussing with business partners or strangers. In the pub the topics you talk about with your colleagues will be different from those you discuss in formal meetings.

Gifts

While gift giving is seen as an important social gesture in some cultures, in others it can be seen as bribery. Most international companies have strict rules on compliance which will limit what you can give and receive as a gift. To save embarrassment, it is worth finding out what these regulations are and making sure that you comply.

In cultures where gifts are acceptable, and even expected, you should make sure that your gift follows cultural norms. Avoid giving a bottle of wine to someone from a culture in which alcohol is forbidden. Don't give a clock to someone in China; this is considered unlucky as the word 'clock' is very close to the word for 'death'. In many cultures it is considered unlucky to give sharp objects like knives or scissors as a gift because they symbolize cutting a relationship.

In some cultures, if you are given a gift, it is considered polite not to open it in front of the giver; this removes the chance of you knowing how much it is worth or being disappointed with it and thus making you or the giver lose face.

Hospitality

How people entertain business partners also varies widely. While in some cultures it is usual to invite business partners to your home, in some cases this can rebound on you. If you are in a poor country living in relative luxury as an expat, your colleagues could interpret an invitation to your home as a sign that you are showing off and may be embarrassed if they feel that they cannot return the hospitality. While in the USA it might be quite normal to invite business partners or casual acquaintances to your home, this does not mean that you are close friends, or even that you will keep in touch with each other.

As far as food and drink are concerned, the key is to make your visitors comfortable. While many people are keen to try local specialities, others are unable to eat particular food for dietary or religious reasons. If you are organizing a meeting with people from many cultures, one way of dealing with different diets is to offer your guests a self-service buffet with a range of food, which is clearly labelled. If you are offered food or drink, it is polite to at least try it, even if you don't like the look of it – you don't have to finish it.

Those involved in sales in particular may find that they are expected to drink large quantities of alcohol. Communal drinking is widely considered to bond people together. If you do intend to drink, make sure that you have eaten enough to absorb the alcohol. If you don't want to drink you can, of course, tell your partners or colleagues that you cannot drink alcohol for health reasons. If you do this, you need to be consistent; don't get caught at the bar enjoying a beer. In meetings provide ice and cold drinks for Americans and hot water or tea for Asian visitors.

What time you arrive for a social engagement also varies. While in some countries it might be normal to arrive at the time mentioned, in others this would be considered rude and the host may still be in the shower if you arrive 'on time'. In the UK people often come 10–15 minutes later than the time mentioned. You might get an invitation which says 7.00pm for 7.30pm which means that you should arrive between 7.00pm and 7.30pm. In Latin America guests commonly arrive much later than the time specified. Check with your host if you are unsure what is expected. See Chapter 5 on tendencies.

Think about the seating arrangements at formal occasions. In China who sits where is decided by the host; you should wait to be seated. Traditionally, it is considered to be an honour to sit on the right of the host. Some visitors to China are surprised by being seated next to someone who cannot speak their language. In this high-context culture it is as important who you are sitting next to as to what you talk about. It is a great privilege to sit next to the senior manager of the company or an important government official even if you can't communicate with them. In some Arab countries men and women may sit in separate rooms in a restaurant or at someone's home.

In countries with a tendency to high collectivism, such as China, many different dishes will be ordered, normally by the host, and everyone will share them. Don't feel that you have to eat all the food – if you do, your host will order more.

If you are in a restaurant with your business partners, you need to think about who is going to pay the bill. The habit of each person paying separately for their meal is restricted to a few countries, like Germany. In many countries the host will pick up the tab or one person will pay the waiter, and the others will divide the bill between them. If you go to the pub in the UK, it is not usual for people to buy drinks individually but to take it in turns to buy a 'round of drinks' from the bar for the whole group.

Other settings

If you are invited to socialize with your business partner, it is normally a good idea to accept the invitation if you possibly can. Socializing can, of course, take place in many different settings. In Finland it might be in the sauna, and some meeting rooms even have sauna facilities close by. In South Korea, the USA and UK it could be a game of golf; the point is not to win or show how good your golf is but to use the change to get to know each other. In Japan an invitation to a bar is not only a chance to get to know your business partners but may be the only way of finding out what they really think, away from the complex dynamics of the formal meeting. The Japanese even distinguish between what is said in official meetings (*tatemae*) and what is said informally (*honne*). An evening spent in the karaoke bar might be more important than spending the time perfecting your presentation for the next day.

Going further

Dignen, B. and McMaster, I. (2013) *Communication for International Business*, London: Collins.
A useful practical guide on English language and communication, designed for native as well as non-native speakers of English.

7

Remotely Together

Global Virtual Collaboration

If you want to go fast, then go alone.

If you want to go far, then let's go together.

African proverb

Key questions
- What challenges do global virtual teams face?
- How can you improve collaboration?

The COVID-19 pandemic dramatically increased the number of people working virtually. For many it was not a choice but forced on them by lockdown. Colleagues and business partners who had previously seen each other every day in the office suddenly faced the challenge of working together remotely from home. Many people who were previously unfamiliar with the technology had to get used to working with virtual communication tools.

This move to virtual working has been coming for some time. As globalization has progressed and technology advanced, so more and more people have been finding themselves working in teams in which they rarely, if ever, have face-to-face contact with fellow team members. The leader is based in the USA, with team members in Shanghai, Dubai and Mumbai. Communication is in international

English, and there are few, if any, physical meetings. Not only are large transnational corporations using globally dispersed teams, but increasingly small- and medium-sized enterprises also see them as a way of tapping talent worldwide and getting closer to their customers and suppliers abroad. There is now a clear trend to the offshoring not only of low-paid work but also of highly skilled roles. Companies are realizing that, if employees can work from anywhere, they can also source employees from anywhere.

While technology can make dispersed work easier, faster and more efficient, virtual global teams need to be carefully managed. When they work well, they create value; when they don't, they demotivate staff and fail to produce the desired results. Space, time and culture are the three variables which impact virtual teams; each can create a gap which needs to be bridged if the team is to succeed.

The advantages

International teams have the potential to be more effective than monocultural teams. A cost-effective way of creating an international team is to work virtually. If you have employees dispersed across the globe, you can turn differences in time zones to an advantage and work 24/7. This delivers a significant benefit for customer services and call centres: English speakers calling from Glasgow don't know if their call is being answered by someone in Cork in Ireland, Bangalore in India or Singapore. Operators are even given training in local accents and popular culture so that they can chat with callers from the UK and USA. The richness of perspectives provided by the diverse team members creates the potential for innovative thinking and solutions, and provides a key to knowing how diverse customers tick: if you want to develop a computer interface for people who are blind, then it helps if you have a person who is blind on the team.

Travel expenses can be reduced dramatically. There are fewer expensive business flights and, even more significantly, a reduction in working time lost while travelling. Executives are relieved of the physical and emotional stress caused by travel, while companies can reduce their carbon footprint at the same time as they contribute to the work-life balance of their employees. Particularly for employees born in Generation Y or later, virtual collaboration is often not a problem at all. They have grown up with it and many prefer virtual to 'real' communication.

The challenges

Although differences in time zones can be an advantage, they also mean that it is very difficult to find times when all colleagues can come together. When one is waking up, the other is going home. Handovers and the transfer of implicit communication (i.e. what is not written down) need to be carefully managed. This can lead to an uneven distribution of information. Those in the physical office communicate more informally with each other than those marginalized on the periphery.

Members of these dispersed teams often complain of isolation. They miss the physical contact and casual encounters in the office. There is also a danger of the regional or local employees losing contact with HQ, 'drifting away' or 'going native'. Local priorities quickly become more important than global targets. Communication problems increase when non-verbal cues are missing. Some complain of 'virtual fatigue' after working online for long periods, and constant intense eye contact can be stressful and intimidating.

Just as intercultural teams can be more effective than monocultural ones, if they are made up of the wrong people or badly managed then they can be much less effective. This is shown in Figure 7.1, which is based on research by Adler (2008). Intercultural teams tend to be either more or less effective than monocultural ones.

Effectiveness of intercultural teams

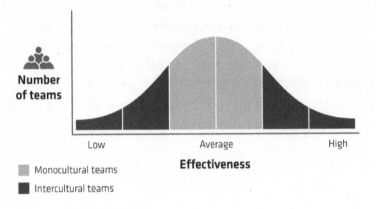

Figure 7.1 Effectiveness of intercultural teams

The key success factors

A useful starting point to optimize the performance of global virtual teams is to look at what makes them successful. Brake (2008) has identified what he calls the 'Six Cs of Global Collaboration':

1. Cooperation: ability to develop and maintain trusting relationships across geographies, time zones and cultures.

2. Convergence: ability to maintain a clear purpose, direction, and shared set of priorities.

3. Coordination: ability to align work through clearly defined roles and responsibilities, shared tools, processes and methods.

4. Capability: ability to leverage the knowledge, skills and experiences of all members, and increase the capabilities of the team as a whole.

5. Communication: ability to generate shared verbal and written understandings across distances via technology.

6. Cultural intelligence: ability to develop and maintain a global virtual workplace inclusive of value and style differences.

Brake's list can be used as a basis for identifying where your team is and what you need to do to make it more effective. This doesn't necessarily mean that you team is failing; it could just be the fine tuning of a powerful machine.

Tips for virtual teams

Select the team to fit the purpose

The first thing to consider is whether an international virtual team is suitable for the task in hand. While it might seem that you can save time and money by using a dispersed or outsourced work-force, it is wise to consider carefully what the real costs will be. You may end up deciding that a monocultural team is best suited to reaching your goals on time. Sharing a common language and cultural background makes it possible to get going quickly, and there will probably be fewer communication problems.

Make sure the goals are clear and shared

To overcome the danger of fragmentation, with different team members pursuing their own goals, it is essential that all team members have a strong sense of purpose and that they are all going in the same direction. The team leader will have to check this at regular intervals and motivate team members to stay on track. Especially when team members have different linguistic backgrounds it is vital that a common understanding of targets and processes is established, checked and maintained throughout the life of a team.

Check everyone knows what their role is

Don't make assumptions about how you think people will see their roles and responsibilities. Different understandings and expectations can be an issue in monocultural teams, but the risk is greater when people from various backgrounds come together in a multicultural team. Even if you all use the same word to describe a role you may well have different interpretations of what this involves: an 'account manager' or 'facility manager' are not the same everywhere.

Check everyone can use the technology

Whether it be a virtual communication tool or a shared database for customer relationship management, it is vital that all team members are able to use the technology. When deciding on which platforms and tools to use make sure that the ones you decide on are accessible in the relevant country. In China, for instance, some applications, which are widely used in other countries, are not available.

Communicate effectively

Exercise 7.1

Look at the example of tips for running a virtual meeting in Figure 7.2. How suitable is it for use in your culture? What might not work when you are working with people from other cultures? A suggested answer can be found at the back of the book.

The Perfect Virtual Meeting?
1. Send an agenda before the meeting.
2. Dress as you would for a face-to-face meeting.
3. Start on time.
4. Agree on meeting rules before you start.
5. Begin with a check-in where participants say how they feel.
6. Ask everyone to have their camera on all the time.
7. Don't do other things during the meeting.
8. Interrupt if people talk about anything not related to the agenda item.
9. End with a check-out where participants say how they feel.
10. Set a date for the next meeting at the end.

Figure 7.2 The perfect virtual meeting?

Exercise 7.2

Ask team members how they would like to communicate with each other. Fill in the communication grid (Figure 7.3) together.

	Exchange information	Brainstorm ideas	Produce documents	Build relationships	Resolve conflicts
Text message	😐	😐	☹️	☹️	☹️
Email	🙂	😐	😐	☹️	☹️
Call	😐	😐	😐	😐	😐
Virtual meeting	🙂	🙂	🙂	😐	😐
Face-to-face meeting	😐	🙂	😐	🙂	🙂

Figure 7.3 Communication grid

This is just one example of what the grid might look like. Make up a unique grid which is customized for use with your team. Whether, for instance, it is feasible to have face-to-face meetings will depend on your location. If the team is widely dispersed, then you will have to think more carefully about having a physical meeting than if you are all in the same office.

When you plan meetings, make sure that you take time zones into account. Vary the times that you hold the meetings to cater for the times in different locations as well as the lifestyles of your team members. Don't make assumptions about when you think is the best time. While for some people an evening meeting may be taboo, for others – for instance single parents with young children – it may be the best time.

Check calendars to find out when there are national and religious holidays. Offices will close in the USA for Thanksgiving, in the UK for Christmas and in China during the Spring Festival.

In Muslim countries, offices operate with reduced working hours during Ramadan and close for Eid al-Fitr. In some countries there will be legal restrictions on when people can be expected to work. In Germany many companies prohibit employees from going to the workplace at the weekend. Remember in some Arab countries the weekend is not Saturday and Sunday but Friday and Saturday – there is a reason why the author of a guide to doing business in the UAE used the title *Don't They Know It's Friday* (Williams, 2017).

Distinguish between what needs to be done synchronously in live-time cooperation and what can be done asynchronously – that is, not at the same time. Add more information about the context and background of a document than you would if the team has regular personal contact.

At the beginning of the meeting allow time for people to 'check in'. Give them time to say where they are, what they are doing and how they are, as well as what they expect from the meeting. If you want to generate ideas or get views from team members who are not so comfortable expressing their views in the whole group, because they are introverted or come from a culture in which this is not appropriate, be sure to make frequent use of the breakout rooms.

Critical incident: Silence is golden

Exercise 7.3

An international company has sites in countries A and B. Representatives from the sites meet virtually to discuss how to improve the way they work together. The discussion turns into a heated debate between the managers from A. The colleagues from B observe the discussion intently but say very little until the chairperson interrupts and turns to one of the team members from B asking 'Did you want to comment on this issue?' They turn off mute, list the key issues on the virtual whiteboard and then make a suggestion for a solution. The others calm down and agree that this solution is the best for all involved.

A suggested answer can be found at the back of the book.

Involve all team members

The Chinese sage Lao-tzu said, 'He who knows does not speak; he who speaks does not know.' While in some cultures periods of silence are appreciated in others silence can make people feel awkward. The diagram shown in Figure 7.4 on turn-taking shows three possible ways of constructing a conversation. In type one the two people speak without interruption or long periods of silence; in type two there are longer silences between the contributions of A and B, and in type three there are overlaps. Tension can occur when someone from type two talks to someone from type three. The type-two person may get frustrated that they don't get a chance to speak; the person from type three might feel that the other has nothing to say. It is up to the chairperson or facilitator of meetings to make sure that everyone can contribute in a way that they are comfortable with. This is especially important in virtual meetings where it is easier to disappear than in face-to-face ones. You may need to invite the quieter or more introverted to contribute or find non-intimidating ways for them to get their voice heard such as writing comments in a chat. The quiet person may have the most valuable ideas.

Turn-taking

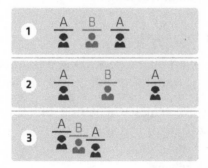

Figure 7.4 Turn-taking

Be careful with brainstorming

Although brainstorming is a common way which many teams use to come up with new ideas there are some challenges that diverse teams face when using it. In his studies of over 55,000 professionals working across 98 countries Livermore (2016) found that attitudes to brainstorming differ widely:

> extroverts who 'think out loud' and Westerners who have grown up in educational environments where classroom participation is required usually thrive in brainstorming sessions. But others around the world grew up in classrooms where they were taught to think before speaking and to avoid standing out with unique ideas. As a result, many individuals in the global workplace dread brainstorming sessions and say very little.

In a US–Chinese team building workshop a US participant answered the question 'What are your strengths?' by saying, 'Thinking out of the box.' The Chinese responded by saying that they thought this was the major weakness of their colleagues who they wished would 'stay in the box'.

Livermore suggests some simple strategies for use when brainstorming with a global team:

- Clearly define the objective.

- Give advance warning so that those who need more time to generate ideas or want to consult others will feel better prepared.

- Insist on 100 per cent participation but provide a variety of ways for input to be provided.

Give and receive feedback

Misunderstandings, which are likely in any human communication, are even more likely when you are communicating across cultures. Communicating virtually without the non-verbal cues from body language and gestures increases the probability of miscommunication and the need for feedback.

In a global organization it is important to find suitable feedback styles which take cultural differences into account. Feedback can, of course, be positive or negative. In some cultures, such as Germany, lack of criticism may be taken as praise and too much praise can be seen as not authentic or unnecessary. For them it is like clapping the pilot when the plane lands safely – you don't clap someone for just doing their job. The Germans have a saying for this: 'Nothing said is praise enough.' In other cultures, like the USA, lack of praise can be seen to imply criticism. Figure 7.5 shows various ways of giving feedback.

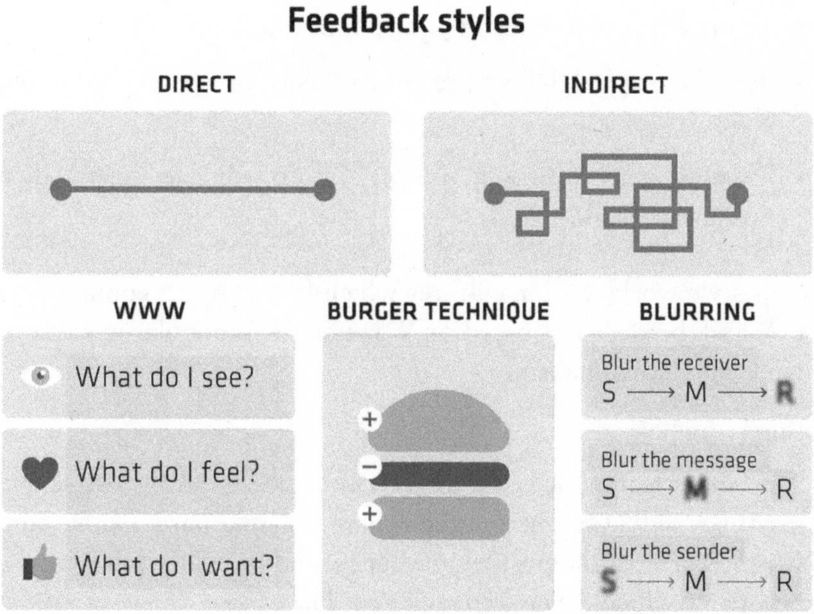

Feedback styles

DIRECT

INDIRECT

WWW

● What do I see?

♥ What do I feel?

👍 What do I want?

BURGER TECHNIQUE

+
−
+

BLURRING

Blur the receiver
S ⟶ M ⟶ **R**

Blur the message
S ⟶ **M** ⟶ R

Blur the sender
S ⟶ M ⟶ R

Figure 7.5 Feedback styles

WWW

A version of this is WWW feedback which involves asking three questions:

1. What do I see?

2. What do I feel?

3. What do I want?

A feature of this style is to use 'I' statements.

- An example of this would be when you want a colleague to concentrate on what you are saying in a meeting to say:

- 'I notice you're looking at your phone a lot.'

- 'It makes me feel that you're not interested in what we're talking about.'

- 'I would ask you to switch it off and do your messaging when we have a break.'

This style works well in cultures which favour direct communication and, because it is based on 'I' messages, is popular in cultures with high individualism.

Burger technique

The burger technique is less direct and combines both positive and negative feedback. The burger consists of two parts of the bun, which represent the positive messages, and the patty which is the negative feedback. The feedback goes like this:

- 'I appreciate your hard work' (*positive*)

- 'There are some financial issues which we need to look at.' (*negative*)

- 'With your positive attitude I am optimistic that we will get back on track.' (*positive*)

You are combining negative feedback, or 'bullets', with positive feedback, or 'bouquets'; it's the 'tickle, slap, tickle' approach. If the receiver of the feedback is used to more direct feedback, then the danger is that they may miss the negative message and go away thinking that everything is fine.

Blurring

If you need to go further on the scale of indirectness, you can use a blurring technique, making your feedback less clear or distinct. From his research into communication patterns in Thailand, Verluyten (1999) identified three ways of criticizing indirectly by using blurring.

Imagine that you have a problem with colleague X coming late to meetings and you are working in a culture in which indirect communication is the norm. You have three options:

1. **Blurring the receiver.** Don't address X directly but say to the whole team, 'We seem to have a problem with punctuality in the group.' You hope that the individual will realize that they are being referred to.

2. **Blurring the message.** Praise X in an overexaggerated way. You hope that they will wonder why you are suddenly heaping the praise on them. An alternative would be to tell a hypothetical story.

3. **Blurring the sender.** Tell X's co-worker that you have a problem with X's punctuality, assuming that they will then pass on the message to X.

When you give feedback don't only think about what you say but also consider when, how and where it happens. Feedback should not be limited to formal staff dialogue sessions but should take place regularly. If there is an emotional situation, it pays to wait until the person has calmed down before talking to them. If the feedback is about something personal or critical, it is better to try to give it face-to-face or on the phone rather than in an email or text message. This is especially important if you are working in a foreign language as there is a greater chance that your message will be misunderstood. It can sometimes help to give feedback outside of the office setting and go for a drink or walk so that you can talk to your colleague more informally. An Indian HR manager reported that, if she had a critical issue with an employee, she would invite them to her home and then raise the topic sometime towards the end of the meal. Beware of using humour, irony or sarcasm as a sweetener for the bitter pill of criticism – if the business partner is used to direct communication, there is an increased chance that your message will get lost or be misinterpreted.

In a virtual team it is easy for some members to take on an unfair share of the work while others disappear conveniently into cyberspace. In a team which regularly meets face-to-face, feedback happens informally – in a virtual team it may be necessary to allocate specific times for feedback sessions.

Foster relationships

Although you may have limited resources and be under pressure to get quick results, if there is a chance for one face-to-face meeting then it is best to have it at the beginning of the project. Team members get to know each other and build trust before they continue to work in a virtual environment. Often this is neglected, and face-to-face meetings have to be arranged later on when things have started to go wrong. It might be too late to repair damaged relationships; prevention is better than firefighting. If team members have met in person, then there is less of a danger that they later on develop a 'virtual persona', a virtual identity which has little to do with their real personality.

If the first meeting of your team is virtual, then make sure that you don't get straight down to business but allow enough time for the team members to get to know each other. To make the diversity of the team concrete, get people to mark where they are on a map of the world.

As an alternative to the classic introduction round of simply going around the group asking people to introduce themselves, ask each team member to prepare a slide with a collage of photographs about themselves. What sort of photographs they post should be left up to them, as what people feel is appropriate and how much personal information they feel comfortable sharing can vary widely. While one person may wish to post pictures of their family, others will prefer to show photographs related to their work. Rather than the person introducing themselves by simply talking about the photographs, you can get the other team members to ask questions.

As teams change over time, it is important to think carefully about how you onboard new team members who join after the project has begun. Make sure they also have a chance to introduce themselves and get to know the rest of the team, familiarize them with the agreed ways of working and give them time to learn how to use any new technology. Provide them with a status report on the progress of the project and assign a mentor to them who can be the first contact in case they need help.

Take time in your virtual meetings to celebrate successes, birthdays and work anniversaries. Just because you are working virtually doesn't mean that all these things you would do face-to-face have to be forgotten.

Build trust

Why people trust someone else varies widely across cultures. While in some cultures trust may be the product of someone's position in the hierarchy, in others trust may be more connected to their perceived competence, or the relationship you have with them. Honesty, appropriate communication and attention to relationships all help to build trust.

Neuroscientific research provides valuable insights into how this works in the brain. Bauer (2008) claims that social acceptance is a fundamental driver for human beings. When we feel appreciated the brain releases oxytocin which makes it possible for us to trust others. Casey and Murphy Robinson (2017) describe it thus:

> Oxytocin is what makes it possible for us to openly move towards others who are different from ourselves and be interested in learning more about them. It is also instrumental in the brain's ability to shift from self-interest to seeing others' interests as important and is shown to boost group-serving behaviour when it is present in the brain.
> Some even call oxytocin 'the love hormone'.

Enjoy the challenge

In effective intercultural teams the team members enjoy working together and find it interesting and enriching to work with people from different backgrounds. They like to talk about the differences, and when these teams meet socially one of the most popular topics of conversation is often culture.

Going further

Brake, T. (2008) *Where in the World is My Team? Making a Success of Your Virtual Global Workplace*, Chichester: Wiley & Sons.
A practical and entertaining guide to working in global virtual teams.
Sigillito Hollema, T. (2020) *Virtual Teams across Cultures: Create Successful Teams Around the World*, Twello, Netherlands: Interact Global.
A practical framework for understanding the dynamics of remote, multi-cultural teams.

8

$1 + 1 = 3$

Inclusive Leadership

He who thinks he is leading and has no one following him is only taking a walk.

Malawian proverb

Key questions

- How does leadership style differ across cultures?
- What are the keys to leading diverse global teams?

Cultural differences and leadership

Although they are closely related, leadership and management are not the same. Leaders have people who follow them, and managers have people who work for them. Leadership is about getting people to believe in a vision and work towards that, while management is operational and includes planning, organizing and coordinating. A line manager will typically have disciplinary control over employees and be involved in making decisions about their compensation and development. Before looking at leadership and management styles in various cultures and at how to be an inclusive leader, think about how you see leadership.

Exercise 8.1

How important do you think it is to have the following qualities in order to be a good leader?

Rate each on a scale of 1–5, where 1 means 'very important' and 5 is 'not important at all'.

A. A high level of specialist knowledge
B. A formal qualification in Business Administration
C. Willingness to ignore hierarchies if this is necessary to get things done
D. Ability to create consensus in the group
E. Willingness to take risks
F. Ability to separate business from personal relationships
G. Clear focus on goals
H. Popularity with employees
I. Charisma
J. A good network of business contacts.

The following cases illustrate different aspects of leading diverse global teams. Suggested answers can be found at the back of the book.

Case: The project team

Exercise 8.2

What is happening here? What could you do as team leader to improve the situation?

You are responsible for a project with team members based on several continents. The targets are challenging and the team needs to perform to a high standard quickly. You have spent a great deal of time planning the project and are disappointed that you are getting very little feedback from the other team members. To try to get everyone on track you have initiated a weekly virtual meeting. Unfortunately, this has not really improved the situation as it is impossible to get them all to attend. Even if they do join the meeting, they normally say very little and just passively agree with any suggestions that you make.

Case: The business plan

Exercise 8.3

A has recently taken over as the manager of an international team. B is a team member. Try to imagine what A and B might be thinking at each stage of the case.

What A said/did	What B said/did	What A thinks	What B thinks
'I have heard that you have a lot of experience with supporting customers who come to us from other countries. If you have a moment then it would be great if you could put together your ideas for me.'			
	'That's true. Fine – I'd be happy to do that.'		
	B didn't have much to do and so prepared some slides on the topic. The next morning she sends them to A.		

'Thanks a lot – that's just what I need for the management meeting this afternoon. This could be a key part of our business plan for next year.'			
	'I didn't realize that it was so urgent. You should have told me.'		
'I thought my instructions were quite clear.'			

Figure 8.1 The business plan

Case: The matrix

Exercise 8.4

What is happening here? What cultural factors could be playing a role? What could the project leader do?

Your international organization has a matrix structure with many people spending most of their time working on projects and reporting to a project leader rather than their disciplinary line manager. You have noticed that, while in your home country this system seems to work extremely well, it is less successful in your new projects in some regions. You have the feeling that the project managers aren't able to get the support needed from project teams in those countries.

Different leadership styles

In a famous study, Laurent (1986) asked managers from different countries if they agreed with the question 'It is important for managers to have at hand precise answers to most of the questions that subordinates may raise about their work.' There were major differences in how people responded with 77 per cent of Japanese, 59 per cent of Italians, 30 per cent of British and 13 per cent of US Americans and Swedes agreeing.

These differences can to some extent be traced back to differences in educational culture in the various countries. In the UK, for instance, it is quite possible to become a manager after having studied arts subjects such as philosophy or ancient languages. This is seen as a general training of the mind, and, after a relatively short period of time at university, the application of this educational experience to the world of work takes place 'on the job'. This is in stark contrast to the system in Germany where more stress is put on obtaining formal qualifications in a technical or business-related subject and where a higher proportion of managers have doctorates than in the UK. This helps to explain why British managers typically see themselves as generalists rather than specialists. Managers interviewed in Argentina considered the most important quality of the manager to be charisma – for them training was considered to be unimportant, as you either have charisma or you don't. The way people see management is, of course, not only influenced by national cultural differences. There can be significant differences within countries as well. In China or Russia it is important to differentiate between former state-run and private enterprises; and in India between traditional family-run businesses and start-ups.

Hierarchies

Hofstede's dimension of power distance gives us a key to understanding differences in attitudes to hierarchy. According to his research companies, Swedish businesses tend to have flatter hierarchies than those in, for instance, India. There are even substantial differences in power distance between neighbouring countries like France and Britain. Table 8.1 shows the results for power distance for selected countries based on the research by Hofstede et al. (2010). The higher the scores are, the higher the distance is between the top and the bottom person in the hierarchy.

Table 8.1   Power distance

Country	Power distance
Sweden	31
Great Britain	35
Germany	35
USA	40
Italy	50
Japan	54
France	68
Brazil	69
India	77

According to Hofstede low power distance cultures are characterized by narrow salary ranges, high degrees of consultation of subordinates and few status symbols. High power distance is associated with wide salary ranges, subordinates being told what to do, and the expectation of privileges and status symbols for managers. Other research shows that in low power distance cultures there is a greater willingness to bypass hierarchical lines than in those with high power distance.

When setting up organizations in other countries it is important to take into consideration these different attitudes to hierarchy – matrix structures which work in one culture will not be effective in countries in which staff tend to expect clear direction from their line manager. In high power distance France managers often see their primary task as controlling whereas in the UK, where power distance is lower, they stress their role as coordinators and use persuasion rather than authority to get people to do things. Attempts to introduce 360-degree feedback, in which subordinates give feedback on the performance of their manager, are likely to fail in cultures with high power distance. One company found that its global system of upward feedback was almost impossible to implement in France. The managers wondered why they should take feedback from employees, and the employees felt it inappropriate to make critical comments on their superiors.

Decision-making

How decision-making works also varies across cultures. Hofstede links his term 'masculinity' with managers being expected to be decisive and assertive and conflicts being resolved by fighting them out. Where the score for masculinity is low, as in Nordic countries, managers strive to create a consensus in the group and conflicts are resolved through negotiation and compromise.

Two different ways of making decisions can be seen in Figure 8.2. In Culture A, a large number of experts are involved in initial detailed and time-consuming planning. Once the plan has been agreed, implementation follows and change, while not impossible, is unlikely. Culture B relies on a series of shorter discussions after which implementation starts; changes are made on the go. For people from Culture B the 'anaylsis paralysis' approach of A seems too slow and cumbersome. On the other hand, those from Culture A feel that the Culture B approach is chaotic and unsystematic. Agile approaches may well appeal to people from Culture B more readily than from those in Culture A where there is high uncertainty avoidance.

Decision-making styles

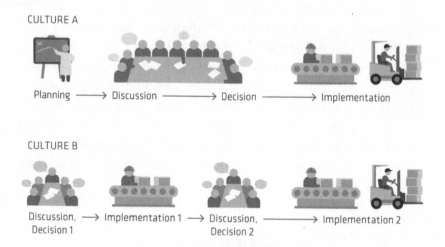

Figure 8.2 Decision-making styles

De Bono (2016) has developed a simple but highly effective method for getting people to think about decision-making from different perspectives which he calls the 'Six Thinking Hats'. The blue hat is for process, the green hat for creativity, the white hat for facts, the yellow hat for benefits, the red hat for feelings and the black hat for cautions. Using this is an easy and effective way of getting people to see an issue from different perspectives, free from any preconceived cultural stereotypes.

Procedures and processes

According to Hofstede, rules and regulations are very important in cultures with strong uncertainty avoidance. Where it is low, there is a belief that no more rules than necessary should be introduced. How many rules are defined also depends on how far the culture favours explicit, or low-context, communication. This may explain the large number of written policies and formal procedures in the USA, despite its relatively weak uncertainty avoidance.

Communication

A French member of an international team working for a US manager complained of the large number of emails they received from the manager packed with information which they considered to be irrelevant to their work. The US manager in turn complained that they were not being kept 'in the loop'. In France with its high power distance, information tends to be seen as power and its formal distribution is often restricted; to compensate for this informal channels of communication are often highly developed.

What is communicated by the manager also varies widely across cultures. Research shows that German managers tend to communicate on tasks whereas in the UK a larger amount of communication centres around motivating staff. Middle managers in the UK tend on average to spend more time talking to employees and in meetings than do those at a similar level in Germany. 'Management by walking around' suggests a management style where it is important for managers to have regular direct contact with their staff. Some French employees with a US manager felt that they weren't being trusted by their manager as he frequently asked them how they were getting on with their project. His intention was quite different – he was indicating the importance of their work and offering his support.

Motivating staff

Managers need to think about how to motivate staff from different cultures. Where uncertainty avoidance is high, job security may be a factor which motivates people to want to work for a company. Celebrating success can be an important part of motivating employees but British, American and French managers of an international computer company when asked how they would celebrate a successful product launch reacted very differently. Whereas the French favoured congratulating the whole team, the British and Americans preferred highlighting individual achievements.

Team development

Although the word 'team' is widely used across the world, it is understood very differently in different cultures. For some, the team is a group of individuals with particular skills and roles and the manager is a team leader because of their ability to coordinate rather than any authority given to them by the organization. For more collectivist cultures, teams will spend a considerable amount of time trying to reach a consensus. When working with teams from other cultures it is also worth clarifying how the team members expect to work together. Is the team there to agree on tasks which are then carried out by individuals working alone or will the tasks be tackled together as a team?

Leaders of international virtual teams should be aware that they need to play different roles at the different stages of a project. The influential model by Tuckman (1965) shows four stages of team development (Figure 8.3).

Four phases of team development

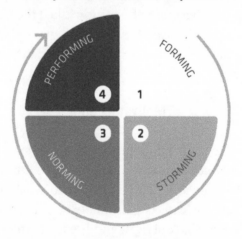

Figure 8.3 Four stages of team development

1. In the **forming** stage the leader has to select the right people for the team and make the goals clear. If the team is expected to create innovative solutions or reflect the needs of a particular customer

segment, then the leader needs to make sure that there is sufficient diversity in the team. While team members are familiarized with the task in hand, those from strongly relationship-oriented cultures will expect to be given adequate time to get to know each other. This time may be difficult to find if there is pressure to get first results quickly.

2. During the **storming** stage the leader will help to facilitate the process of the team members getting to know each other and developing mutual trust. At this stage it is important that cultural differences are made explicit; team members need to get to know each other's working styles. If this stage is neglected, then there is an increased likelihood of conflict later on. It is very important that the team leader encourages the exchange of different opinions and styles so that they are brought out into the open.

3. The next stage, **norming,** involves all team members agreeing on and committing to the common task and way of working.

4. When it comes to **performing** the team leader will concentrate on maintaining trust and monitoring results.

Later Tuckman and Jensen (1977) added a fifth stage which they called **adjourning** which includes completing the task and then breaking up the team. During this phase the leader needs to concentrate on wrapping up the project and celebrating success in a culturally appropriate way. In agile teams, as found in software development, **swarming** takes place: groups come together frequently and informally to solve a problem. Roles are fluid and often change.

Situational leadership

To bridge culture gaps the leader will take on a number of roles including facilitating, translating ideas, interpreting concepts, integrating team members, mediating in disputes and empathetic comforting of dissatisfied or unmotivated members of the team. You need to fit the style to the situation in which you find yourself and to the cultural background of your team members. A useful model which is suitable for use with intercultural teams is known as situational leadership, first developed by Hersey and Blanchard (1969). Figure 8.4 shows four types of leadership according to the degree of employee and task orientation.

Situational leadership

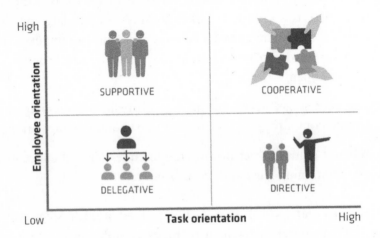

Figure 8.4 Situational leadership

The *delegative* leadership style means that responsibility is to a large extent delegated to the employee who is supposed to take the initiative. The manager will not get involved in the details. In the case of the *supportive* leadership style the manager will take into account the wishes of the employee who is the focus of attention. They will encourage the employee whenever they can. In the case of *directive* leadership style detailed instructions are provided by the manager. With the *cooperative* leadership style the manager and employee work closely together to find solutions.

The following real-life case illustrates some important issues which may occur in an international team.

Case: The binational team

Exercise 8.5

What cultural factors are playing a role here? What are your recommendations for improving the collaboration? A suggested answer can be found at the back of the book.

Background information

On the surface the highly successful joint venture in the electronics industry is going well. R&D is based in several sites in country A and production in country B; the business is starting to be profitable. When tensions emerge in the team an external consultant is brought in to analyse the situation. This is what she reports after interviewing representatives from both sides.

The manager from country A on the team from country B:

We are impressed by our ambitious colleagues and their speedy reactions. They seem keen to learn and are very open-minded. What is not so good is that they aren't prepared to take responsibility or willing to follow agreed procedures. They think in a hierarchical way, and there is very little horizontal communication. They seem reluctant to take the initiative or make independent decisions. Recently, they have started to turn up late to meetings or not appear at all. When we ask them about a problem they often circle around the point, and it is very difficult to know what they are really thinking. They smile politely and say 'yes' but don't do anything. I wish they'd put the cards on the table and tell us directly if they have a problem with something.

We've hired quite a few new colleagues from B, but although they have excellent paper qualifications we've been disappointed with their performance. The other issue is loyalty. We hire them, train them up, and then they leave and join one of our competitors.

The manager from country B on the team from country A:

They are excellent planners and think very logically. We like their focus on quality and their disciplined straightforward approach. They like our country and obviously enjoy themselves when they come to see us.

On the other hand, they don't trust us. They don't give us any real responsibility and lay down complicated processes which just slow everything down and stop us from reaching our targets. They waste time with too many meetings. They are never available when we need them – you can't get hold of them in the evening or at the weekend, and they always seem to be away on holiday. If we can't get an answer to our questions quickly, then we have a problem with the deadlines that they keep insisting on.

Some of our team have been shocked by the way they behave in their free time. Maybe there are too many temptations in our city. They complain about us stealing know-how but at the same time when they have a few hours free before their flight home they make a beeline for the fake market and buy watches and fashion accessories for their family and friends.

Inclusive leadership

Increased diversity of teams requires a new type of leadership which is radically different from the traditional role of the line manager. Bourke (2016) describes this as 'inclusive leadership'. This involves:

Treating people and groups fairly – that is, based on their unique characteristics, rather than on stereotypes.

Personalizing individuals – that is, understanding and valuing the uniqueness of diverse others while also accepting them as members of the group.

1 + 1 = 3

Leveraging the thinking of diverse groups for smarter ideation and decision making that reduces the risk of being blindsided.

According to Bourke, inclusive leaders are 'highly committed to diversity and inclusion, have the courage to speak up and challenge the status quo, are mindful of personal and organisational blind spots, are curious, are culturally intelligent and able to leverage the thinking of diverse groups'.

Going further

Comfort, J. and Franklin, P. (2014) *The Mindful International Manager: How to Work Effectively across Cultures*, 2nd edn, London: Kogan Page.
A guide to managing across cultures which encourages observation and reflection.
De Bono, E. (2016), *Six Thinking Hats: Run Better Meetings, Make Faster Decisions*, London: Penguin Life.
A tried-and-tested approach to making decisions and exploring by thinking in different ways.
Guida, R., Trickey, D. and Fregnan, E. (2015) *Managing Challenges across Cultures: A Multicultural Project Team Toolbox*. Milan: McGraw Hill Education.
A highly practical guide to managing diverse projects with many useful activities and tools.
Krogerus, M., and Tschäppeler, R. (2011) *The Decision Book: Fifty Models for Strategic Thinking*, London: Profile Books.
A useful collection of decision-making models which can be used in different cultural settings.

Oiling the Works

Influencing to Win

Build your opponent a golden bridge to retreat across.

Sun Tzu

Key questions

- How can you influence people even if you don't have formal authority?
- How do negotiations and conflict resolution differ in different cultures?

Case: Global data

Exercise 9.1

- The case describes a typical situation which you might face in a global organization.
- What cultural factors could be playing a role? What could be done to improve the situation?

You are the global sales manager of a company with operations in many countries worldwide. One of your most important tasks is to collate the sales figures from the regions and present them to top management. You frequently have problems getting data from the regional sales teams, and if you do get it you sometimes wonder how accurate it is. You are concerned about this as it is the basis of all business

> decisions and needs to be high quality and delivered on time. The responsibility to deliver the data is clearly stated in the job descriptions of the regional sales managers.
>
> A suggested answer can be found at the back of the book.

Influencing techniques

Just as there is not just one leadership style which can be used in all cultural settings so there is no one-size-fits-all way of influencing people. You need to have a range of different influencing styles in your intercultural toolkit, as well as the skill to use the right one, with the right people, at the right time, in the right place. Most people feel comfortable with one or two techniques, but if you want to influence diverse groups of people you may need to move out of your comfort zone and try using techniques which you don't normally use. There are two main types of influencing techniques:

- **Push techniques** involve putting external pressure on people to do things. This can mean appeal to power, regulations or rational persuasion. Arguments like, 'You must do it because the boss wants it to happen' is suited to working in high power distance cultures. In universalist cultures with a strong belief in rules, you can say: 'We have to do it because of the compliance regulations.' Rational persuasion would involve saying: 'We must do this because it makes sense.'

- **Pull techniques** involve appealing to values, expertise or relationships. Examples of this are a belief in quality, sustainability or health and safety: 'We should do this because it will reduce our carbon footprint.' Appealing to expertise would mean, 'We should do this because the expert says so.'

Appealing to relationships is crucial for success in high relationship-oriented cultures. *Guanxi*, or social networks of power, are central to doing business in China; over their lifetime Chinese people culti-vate a complex web of relationships which are bound together by mutual obligations. You need this network if you want to get things done. As a result, the outsider who doesn't have access to the network or 'ingroup collective' will find it extremely difficult to do business. They need to work through an intermediary who can make the necessary connections.

Negotiating

Just as cultural factors are important when you want to influ-ence people so they must be taken into account at every stage of a negotiation.

1 Preparation

When preparing to present your products or services it pays to think carefully about the cultural background of your customers. In some cultures, people will expect a sales presentation to focus on detailed information about the product or service while in others they may well want to see the 'big picture' before getting down to details. One way of finding out about this is to observe how other people in the target culture speak to their customers.

In future-oriented cultures the convincing arguments in the sales pitch will be the ones that focus on future benefits. Customers from past-oriented cultures will expect to hear about the history and past achievements of your company.

2 Exchanging information and building trust

It's worth finding out the answers to some basic questions before you start negotiating. Where will the negotiations take place: in the office, in a restaurant, on a golf course, in the sauna, at some-one's home, in a pub or maybe even in a karaoke bar? Who should be present? In cultures with high power distance it is essential that not only the technical experts but also senior managers are present even if they lack relevant technical knowledge.

A key to negotiating is the ability to build trust. In relationship-oriented cultures trust will develop from being related to someone, knowing someone or being recommended by someone. In task-oriented cultures trust may be based on a person's qualifications, perceived competence or track record.

3 Bargaining

It is important to find out what the bargaining style of your business partner is. How far is your asking price away from the desired price? While in 'craftsman cultures' the price is closely linked to quality and there is little scope for negotiation, in 'merchant cultures' there will be more room for manoeuvre.

When do you start talking about price? Is it early on in negotiations or only after you have had a chance to assess the precise requirements of the customers? The thinking behind the first approach is that there is no point in wasting time talking about the details if the price is out of scope, while the second approach is based on the idea that the supplier needs to know precisely what the customer wants in order to estimate what it will cost.

4 Closing and commitment

What does the contract mean? Is it more of an expression of intent to work together which can change when circumstances change or is it a detailed agreement which has to be strictly adhered to? Western business people are often shocked when negotiating in China and their business partners sign a contract but want to renegotiate when circumstances change.

Dealing with conflict

Ury (1991) describes how to deal with conflict situations when negotiating. He sees five ways of 'breaking through the impasse'. These are especially useful for intercultural negotiations.

1. **'Don't react: go to the balcony.'** If people are emotional then they will not be open to logical arguments. So it can help to take a break and a step back from the situation and take time to think about what is going on.

2. **'Don't argue: step to their side.'** Listen actively to the other person and acknowledge them and their arguments.

3. **'Don't reject: reframe.'** Ask probing questions and try to change the frame of the conversation.

4. **'Don't push: build them a golden bridge.'** Start from where the other person is and look for interests that can be met.

5. **'Don't escalate: use power to educate.'** Show the consequences of not reaching an agreement. Show the other person a way out which will satisfy both parties.

Active listening

Non-aggressive communication is another key to avoiding conflicts. Rosenberg (1999) calls this 'nonviolent communication'; one key aspect of this is active listening. Listening is not the passive activity that many people assume it to be. When we listen we are responding to the other person, even if we don't say anything. We indicate our reaction through non-verbal signals and by asking questions. Often though, particularly in conflict situations, people switch off and aren't really listening at all but waiting with a loaded pistol ready to shoot a clever response.

Active listening involves listening with complete uninterrupted engagement, concentrating on the facts but also finding out more and building a relationship. To listen actively you need to do the following:

- **Reflect feelings.** Say things like, 'I can understand that you are disappointed with the service'. This makes people feel that you understand them.

- **Reformulate.** Check that you have understood facts and intentions. 'So, in other words ...'

- **Clarify.** Check that you have understood the details. 'What exactly do you mean by ...?

- **Ask open questions.** Avoid closed questions which can be answered by 'yes' or 'no'; instead use open ones like 'Tell me more about ...'

- **Summarize.** 'Let me recap on what we discussed.' This 'echo effect' can strengthen rapport.

All this should not be a mechanical process. You need to be genuinely interested in what the other person is saying and show that interest. You do this through non-verbal signals like eye contact or nodding your head or verbally by using reinforcing phrases like, 'Yes, I see'. Remember to make sure that your body language is culturally appropriate (see Chapter 5). Your posture should mirror the posture of the other person, but beware of trying to manipulate them by over consciously using mirroring techniques; the other person may well pick up on this, and if you are not interested, 'body leakage' will reveal your true feelings. If you say, 'I have plenty of time' and at the same time are looking at your watch or phone, then the real message is that you are in a hurry.

Case: The negotiation

Exercise 9.2

What do you think is happening here? What cultural factors could be playing a role?

The sales team from A had high hopes for their trip to country B, the purpose of which was to sell industrial equipment for an assembly line. The meeting with the customer from country B seemed to be going well and they appeared to be

---

interested, but to the surprise of the team from country A the customer kept asking about prices before they had said exactly what they wanted:

'To give you a proper quotation we need to analyse your precise requirements. When we've got this information and checked with our commercial team, we'll get back to you as soon as we can. If you fill in the spreadsheet with your requirements by next Monday we can make you an offer by Friday. Is that OK for you?' said the leader of the sales team from A. 'Yes, that's fine,' replied the customer from B.

The team from A was disappointed when they didn't get the information they needed and heard that the customer was negotiating with a different supplier.

A suggested answer can be found at the back of the book.

Conflict

Even if we do our best to avoid it, conflict is inevitable. It is often seen as something negative but it can have positive results: the storm is necessary to clear the air.

Glasl (1999) describes how conflict can escalate in nine stages from light tension to destruction.

1. Hardening. Differences of opinion develop.

2. Debate and polemics. Discussion turns to verbal confrontation.

3. Actions, not words. Belief that actions not words will resolve the issue.

4. Images and coalitions. Focus is not on the issue at stake but winning the conflict.

5. Loss of face. Attacks become personal.

6. Strategies of threat. Resort to threats.

7. Limited destructive blows. Parties try to harm each other.

8. Fragmentation of the enemy. Attempts to destroy the opponent who is now the enemy.

9. Together into the abyss. Self-destruction is accepted. In intercultural interactions it is important to bear in mind that the way conflict is expressed varies widely. Where there is a tendency towards direct communication, the conflict will be clear for all to see with 'the cards on the table'. Where there is indirect communication and in a high-context culture, the conflict may be indicated by a change of mood, silence or simply failure to turn up to meetings.

Face

Although no one wants to 'lose face' the concept of face plays a more major role in some cultures than others. Face refers to the position, status and image of an individual in society. It is especially important in China where hierarchy, social roles and relationships are central to doing business. Face can be 'given', 'lost' and 'saved'. If you are invited by your Chinese manager to a team dinner on a Friday evening after work, you are strongly advised to go. Even if it might be inconvenient, or you have already planned to do something else, it is an important chance to 'give your manager face'. If you don't go, it may even be understood as a signal that you want to distance yourself from the team.

Resolving conflict

To de-escalate conflict, you may need to get external help. The type of help which is effective will depend on the stage of the conflict as well as the culture of those involved. At the early stages the conflict may be resolved by the protagonists themselves, although even at this stage in high power distance cultures people may want to get someone senior in the hierarchy involved. In the later stages of conflict there will be an increase in the need for external help, which can range from support from a team member to a professional mediator.

Think about conflict resolution by reflecting on this example.

Exercise 9.3

There is one orange and two people both want it. What do you do?

Figure 9.1 shows various options for reacting to this or any other conflict.

Conflict resolution

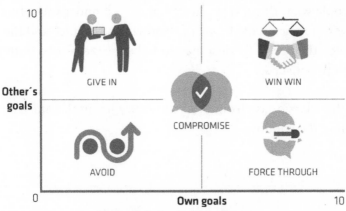

Figure 9.1 Conflict resolution

The axes indicate how far you are oriented towards fulfilling your own goals and how far you are oriented towards fulfilling the goals of the other. There are basically five possible approaches:

1. **Avoid.** This means doing nothing or 'sweeping the conflict under the carpet'.

2. **Give in.** You are submissive and accept the goals of the other.

3. **Force through.** You force the other person to accept your goals.

4. **Compromise.** Each party steps down from their maximum demands.

5. **Win-Win.** This involves finding an optimal solution for both sides.

This model can be applied to the dilemma with the orange:

- The **0/0 position** means that neither person gets the orange.

- The **0/10 and 10/0 positions** mean that one person gets it.

- The **5/5 position** would involve each person getting half of the orange.

- The **10/10 position** could involve finding out why the two people want the orange. Ideally, they will find a way of meeting both of their needs. If one of them wants the juice and the other needs the peel – for instance to bake a cake – then both needs can be satisfied.

Another classic case from everyday office life in the office is about opening the window.

Critical incident: The window

Exercise 9.4

What can you do?

> Two co-workers share an office. One likes to have fresh air and prefers to have the window open most of the time, complaining that they feel sleepy and can't work well if the window is closed. The other is sensitive to draughts which they say gives them a stiff neck.

A suggested answer can be found at the back of the book.

Being unconditionally constructive

Whether trying to influence people, negotiate or solve conflicts, Fisher and Brown (1989) advocate being 'unconditionally constructive'. This means accepting that others will see things differently and express themselves in different ways to you, but always trying to look beyond fixed positions to find common interests. Listen actively to others to make sure that you really understand their position, even if you disagree with it, constantly check your own ideas against observable facts, try to save face and avoid emotional outbursts, blaming, judging and labelling others on the basis of negative stereotypes.

Going further

Fisher, R. and Brown, S. (1989) *Getting Together: Building Relationships As We Negotiate*, New York: Penguin.
A deeper look at what it means to be 'unconditionally constructive' and build relationships in negotiations.
LeBaron, M. and Pillay, V. (2006) *Conflict across Cultures: A Unique Experience of Bridging Differences*. Boston, MA: Intercultural Press.
Powerful stories about resolving conflict across cultures by contributors from Canada, South Africa, Japan and the USA.
Ury, W. (1991) *Getting Past No: Negotiating in Difficult Situations*. New York: Bantam Books.
The classic guide to negotiating by one of the authors of *Getting to Yes*.

10

The Roller Coaster

Managing Global Change

When you enter a village, obey the village.

Japanese proverb

Key questions

- How can you make global change projects work?
- How do cultural factors impact cross-border mergers and acquisitions?

While it is clear that cultural differences can be important for individuals and teams the impact on organizations are even greater. Gibson et al. (2003) describe this as 'Return on Culture'. This applies whether you are setting up a production site or a sales office overseas, harmonizing global processes, a partner in a cross-border joint venture or involved in international mergers and acquisitions (M&A). These activities are challenging enough when carried out in a familiar environment but are even more difficult when they take place internationally. To be successful, cultural factors need to be considered at every stage of the change process.

Transforming organizations

Many organizations focus on rules, regulations, tools and processes when trying to transform themselves. Top management makes a decision, issues a circular and assumes that things will now change in the way that it wants. What it all too often fails to do is to address the 'soft factors', the different attitudes and values which act as barriers to change.

Change processes follow a predictable course. The first reaction of employees is shock and denial. This can be the result of our natural bias towards the status quo. As the neuroscientists Fleming et al. (2010) point out the default mode of the brain is to reject change:

> When faced with a complex decision, people tend to accept the status quo, as reflected in the old adage, 'When in doubt, do nothing.' Indeed, across a range of everyday decisions, such as whether to move house or trade in a car, or even whether to flip the TV channel, there is a considerable tendency to maintain the status quo and refrain from acting.

After the initial rejection comes frustration and anger which can lead into the 'valley of tears'. At this stage many change projects fail completely. If there is a turnaround and people start to experiment with the new ideas and then decide to engage positively, then there is a chance that the changes will be integrated into the organization. The idea of the change process as an emotional roller coaster is illustrated in the curve based on the work of Kübler-Ross and Kessler (2014), which was originally designed to show people's reactions to the death of a loved one.

The next question that arises is how we can manage change. Kotter (1996 and 2014) identifies eight steps:

1. **'Create a sense of urgency'** – identifying opportunities and risks.

2. **'Build a guiding coalition'** – getting together people powerful enough to drive the change.

3. **'Form a strategic vision'** – creating a vision shared by the team.

Change curve

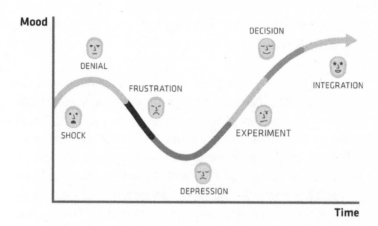

Figure 10.1 Change curve

4. **'Enlist a volunteer army'** – communicating the vision and using all means to spread it in the organization.

5. **'Enable action by removing barriers'** – empowering others to act on the vision.

6. **'Generate short-term wins'** – making sure that there are short-term benefits and rewarding those who help bring them about.

7. **'Sustain acceleration'** – consolidating improvements.

8. **'Institute change'** – communicating the connections between new behaviour and change.

A real-life example illustrates some of the sorts of cultural factors that have to be taken into account when managing an international change project. It concerns an ambitious attempt to standardize a key HR process.

Case: The global HR process

Exercise 10.1

What cultural factors do you think need to be considered when rolling out this process globally?

An international company plans to standardize its performance management process for employees worldwide. The process consists of a number of steps including target setting, monitoring of employee performance, appraisal meetings, as well as a round table of managers and HR to decide on compensation and development measures, as well as feedback meetings between managers and employees to present the results and plan implementation. The system has worked well in selected countries and is to be introduced globally to increase the transparency of the talent pool and foster global mobility.

A suggested answer can be found at the back of the book.

Mergers and acquisitions (M&A)

According to Kenny (2020) between 70 and 90 per cent of acquisitions fail. Most fail to achieve synergies, and some, far from creating value, destroy it. Despite this fact, mergers and acquisitions remain one of the main strategic tools for companies to gain new markets and know-how.

When the pressure is on and a large number of financial and legal issues have to be dealt with, it is all too easy to neglect the 'soft' or 'people' factors. If such factors are not taken into account, this will soon become clear from loss of staff and customers, an inefficient supply chain, organizational confusion, and wasteful duplication of products and services. To prevent this, it is essential to take cultural factors seriously at all stages of the M&A process by:

- **Identifying your approach.** Think carefully about the best way of getting into the new market. Is it better to take over a local company and leverage its knowledge, or to take advantage of possible subsidies and tax breaks to set up your own operation but with the risk of problems arising from lack of local knowledge?

- **Cultural due diligence.** Alongside financial due diligence you will need to carry out a culture audit. Think carefully about all types of culture involved. Corporate as well as national and regional cultures need to be taken into account.

- **Strategy and vision.** What are the visions and strategies of the companies involved? Look carefully at company websites, logos and mission statements.

- **Management style.** How far do the management styles match or complement each other?

- **Decision-making.** Can the board of directors of your target company make decisions independently, or is there a supervisory board which has to approve them? Can managers make decisions, or is there a need for consensus as will be the case in low power distance cultures?

- **Hierarchy.** How many levels of hierarchy are in the target company? How far is this compatible with your existing structures?

- **Sales channels.** What are the channels to market? How far do they fit in or add to channels that you already have?

- **HR policies.** What determines the compensation of employees? How much job security is there? How far is this regulated by national legislation and how far by company policy? How difficult will it be to relocate staff or reduce the workforce? What role do trade unions and workers' representatives play?

- **Communication.** A key to success is effective communication with all the stakeholders. These can include customers, employees, management, suppliers, trade unions, workers' councils, shareholders, government and local authorities as well as the general public.

To change a company you are acquiring or merging with it is essential to understand the cultural roots. At the same time it is important not to overestimate the effect of cultural differences. There is a danger that, if you are deeply interested in culture, you may look to culture as the explanation for everything that happens. As the saying goes, 'If all you have is a hammer, everything looks like a nail.' It can be convenient to blame national cultural differences when things go wrong to cover over the fact that sometimes people just make bad business decisions.

The following case illustrates what can happen when neighbouring countries are involved in M&A. Often, people assume that because they are so geographically close or share the same language cultural factors will not be important. Don't fall into the trap of similarity: subtle differences can have unexpected impact.

Case: Close neighbours

Exercise 10.2
- What is happening here?
- What would you recommend that the management does?

As is common in such cases, HQ in country A installed a management from its own country into the company in country B which it had just acquired. It thought it was important to provide a strong link with the rest of the company and so speed up the integration process. It was essential to introduce standard

---

procedures as quickly as possible so that the new acquisition could pay off and contribute its share to the business.

Interviews with the employees from country B revealed a number of areas of concern. One of the main ones was that communication with the management from country A was unsatisfactory. When the managers heard about this, they immediately took action and arranged for employees to be invited in small groups for coffee each day to discuss issues of importance. Several months later, after almost all employees had attended the 'coffee and chat sessions', the workforce was still complaining about bad communication.

A suggested answer can be found at the back of the book.

Glocalization

When transforming global organizations the central question is how far to localize and how far to standardize. The various options are shown in Figure 10.2, which is based on the dilemma reconciliation technique developed by Hampden-Turner and Trompenaars (2000). A common conclusion is to say that you need to think global and act local. HSBC, 'the world's local bank', used this as the focus of its highly successful advertising campaign.

At one extreme, you can try to standardize globally – if taken to the extreme, you could call this 'colonize': you introduce your ideas and take little account of local differences. The other extreme is to 'go native': you do as little standardization as possible and let the local companies decide what suits them best. A middle position might be summed up as 'When in Rome, do as the Romans do': have a global approach, change in a limited way when dealing with the regions, and change back when you return home. Not being active at all is labelled 'stay at home'. The most promising position is to create genuine 'synergies' through combining the

Global and local

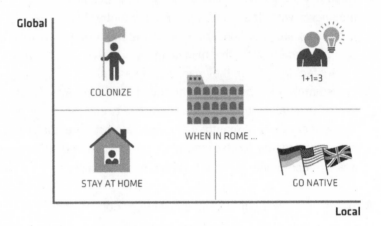

Figure 10.2 Global and local

strengths of the different cultures: the whole becomes more than the sum of the parts ('1 + 1 = 3'). To achieve this is the ultimate challenge for constructive intercultural management.

A concrete example of this is provided by van Boeijen and Zijlstra (2020) in their discussion of what glocalization means for design:

> A strategy to bridge two different cultures through design could be to combine products from both cultures and translate the result into a new product category. One example is the burkini, which combines the burka with a bikini, while another is Bollywood, which combines Bombay with Hollywood.

Methods

As more and more companies face the challenges of transforming organizations, so the range of methods available to support this is developing rapidly. Commonly used methods for change management programmes include:

- needs analysis using interviews and online surveys
- management workshops
- a communication plan
- employee events
- integration workshops
- coaching of management
- regular 'pulse checks' to gauge the mood of the workforce.

To get away from top-down change management there are some dynamic approaches which seek to mobilize the workforce from the grassroots.

Action learning

Reg Revans, the pioneer behind action learning, was inspired by the story of the sinking of the Titanic in 1912. His father was a marine surveyor and was involved in interviewing surviving crew after the tragedy. Investigations showed that the lack of a feedback culture was one of the major causes of the disaster. People knew that things were wrong, but didn't speak up or were not heard. Pedler (2008) describes how the idea behind action learning is to activate the employees to address the real 'wicked' issues. Small groups, called action learning 'sets', meet and discuss the issues faced by the members of the group; each session ends with concrete action items. Although this method has proven to be a powerful way of involving many people in organizations, it does, however, require a setting in which everyone has the time, space and permission to come up with grassroots solutions to problems. It may not be so easy to implement in high power distance cultures.

Hot spots

To bring about change and innovation in organizations Gratton (2007) focuses on what she calls 'hot spots':

Hot spots are crucial to organisational health. Hot spots occur when our energy and excitement are inflamed through an igniting question or a vision of the future. Hot spots come about through a co-operative mindset, the ability to span boundaries, and an igniting purpose. The lack of any one of these three elements significantly reduces the potential energy of a hot spot. The capacity of this potential energy to be translated into productive energy – and hence innovation and value creation – is dependent on the productive capacity of the people within the emerging hot spot.

Viral Change™

The thinking behind this approach developed by Herrero (2008) is that we are most influenced by our peers. At school, children want to fit in and copy the behaviour of other pupils and the same is true in the workplace. The key to this approach is to identify the influencers in an organization and convince them of the new behaviours which you want to propagate. They are then given the structure and support to spread the new culture. There can be resistance to this way of working in high power distance cultures when managers are used to a directive style and reluctant to step back into the role of a 'backstage' manager.

Working Out Loud

According to Stepper (2020):

> Working Out Loud is a way to build relationships that help you achieve a goal, develop a skill, or explore a new topic. Instead of networking to get something, you invest in relationships by making contributions over time, including your work and experiences that you make visible.

This can be very appealing to relationship-oriented cultures.

Deep Democracy

Deep Democracy, sometimes known as the Lewis Method, is a vision and a method developed by Myrna Lewis and originated from the transition period in South Africa as it transformed from apartheid to democracy. Kramer (2021) describes its key feature:

> [Deep Democracy] enables all voices to be heard. Inevitably, there will be differences of opinion amongst people. The Lewis Method has unique tools, which enable these differences to be resolved and to gain the wisdom that lies within the collective views. This leads to innovative and creative solutions and enhanced relationships.

A key success factor is making sure that the methods you choose are appropriate and effective in the cultures in which you are working. Think about the origin of these methods and where they have been used successfully. Although *kaizen* (continuous improvement), just-in-time (JIT), empowerment and agile change management methods can all work in different cultural environments, don't assume that just because an approach works in the USA or the UK it will automatically also work in China or India. If you feel that the method will be quite different from what people are used to, it doesn't mean that you have to abandon the idea of using it. You may just need to sell it harder to your target group – maybe the different approach is what they have been waiting for.

Going further

Gratton, L. (2007) *Hot Spots: Why Some Companies Buzz with Energy and Innovation – and Others Don't*, Harlow: Pearson.
An introduction to the ideas of innovation hot spots which will drive change in organizations.

Herrero, L. (2008) *Viral Change™: The Alternative to Slow, Painful and Unsuccessful Management of Change in Organisations*, 2nd edn, Meeting Minds.
An approach to spreading change through the influence of peers.
Pedler, M. (2008) *Action Learning for Managers*. Farnham: Gower.
A concise practical guide to action learning by a leading practitioner.
Stepper, J. (2020) *Working Out Loud: A 12-Week Method to Build New Connections, a Better Career, and a More Fulfilling Life*, Vancouver: Page Two.
A dynamic method for mobilizing the workforce for personal and organizational change.
Trompenaars, F. and Prud'homme van Reine, P. (2004) *Managing Change across Corporate Cultures*, Chichester: Capstone Publishing.
Examines the role of corporate culture differences in change processes.

11

The Barometer

Coping with International Assignments

How shall I talk of the sea to the frog,

If it has never left its pond?

How shall I talk of the frost to the bird of the summer land,

If it has never left the land of its birth?

How shall I talk of life with the sage,

If he is a prisoner of his doctrine?

Zhuang Zhou

Key questions
- What are the opportunities and risks of working abroad?
- What can you and your company do to make your international assignment successful?

Exercise 11.1
Imagine a colleague is planning to go on a three-year assignment abroad. They will be travelling with their family. What advice would you give them ...
- before they depart?
- while they are away?
- before they return?
- after they return?

The international assignment

You are excited. You have the opportunity to work abroad for three years. You know that this will be an important step in your international career. Of course, the job will be demanding, but it all sounds too good to be true. If your international assignment is to be a success, it pays to be aware of some common pitfalls.

There are various types of international assignment. A short-term posting lasts up to two years, with long-term delegations typically being three to five years. Anything longer may lead to a permanent transfer. Of course, global mobility also includes business travel for a few days or weeks, regular cross-border commuting, project work and international transfers and hiring. Staff given such assignments all face common challenges as well as unique issues connected with the type of assignment.

For an international company, sending key staff for a period abroad is important for strategic business reasons, as well as part of the development of employees. It is, however, extremely expensive. The costs for the delegate and their family include relocation, housing allowances, language courses and school fees, as well as the hidden costs caused by the limited effectiveness of the employee while they are adjusting to the foreign culture. It pays off for companies to be careful about who they send on these assignments and to invest in effective support at all stages of the delegation.

Cultural adjustment

Although the term 'culture shock' has been around since the 1960s and is still in common usage, it is perhaps more helpful to talk about 'cultural adjustment'. Just as the metaphor of the iceberg is too static and rigid to properly illustrate the fluidity of culture (see Chapter 1), so the idea of a dramatic and fixed cycle of experience for expatriation needs to be replaced with something which better reflects the diversity of experience that people have when living and working abroad.

Although for many people working internationally is highly enriching, it is important not to underestimate the stress put on individuals by the global workplace. Company doctors and therapists report of burnt-out executives suffering from the psychological and physical effects of travel and intercultural encounters. The exact extent of this is difficult to determine as many sufferers deny their condition or are unwilling to admit that they don't have everything under control for fear of damaging their career prospects. Travel to 'difficult countries' and extended assignments abroad are frequently a prerequisite for senior management positions.

HR and global mobility professionals are increasingly looking for ways of preventing and treating everything from jet lag and 'culture shock' to the post-traumatic depression connected to experiences while working in extreme situations. Families and co-workers also need to find ways of supporting loved ones and colleagues in these challenging environments.

Although it is too dramatic and static a term for what most people experience, it is useful to look the term 'culture shock' as used by Oberg (1960) in the 1960s. According to him, it has six main features:

- strain caused by adapting to the new culture

- a sense of loss of friends, status and possessions

- being rejected by people from the new culture

- confusion about roles, expectations, feelings and identity

- fear of cultural differences

- feeling of not being able to cope.

Some say that culture shock is like being a 'fish out of water'. Depending on who you are and where you come from, you might find some situations in different cultures extremely stressful. Of course, the effects of these situations on you will also depend on your level of sensitivity and what your role is. Are you just passing through as a tourist, or are you on a long-term assignment during which the cumulative effects of experiencing stressful situations will be considerable?

Here are some real-life examples of extreme situations collected from employees working in various roles in a number of countries:

- 'While I was driving to work, I had to drive past the site of a car accident. The driver had been killed but no one removed the body for ages. I had to drive past there twice a day.'

- 'We were meeting in a luxurious hotel – the food was excellent but there was simply too much for us to eat at the buffet. The leftovers were simply thrown away. It was terrible to see the waste and then go outside and witness the extreme poverty in the slums.'

- 'I felt so stupid in the supermarket. I couldn't believe that I had to pay for the shopping cart. Then at the cash desk they didn't accept my credit card. As I don't speak the language, I couldn't talk to the cashier. No one was there to pack my shopping, and they even wanted me to pay extra for a plastic bag. This is just a trivial thing but was one of a series of frustrations that I had experienced since I arrived. It was all getting too much. I felt terrible when I broke into tears in front of my children.'

- 'During an international aid project we drove through the country in a convoy. Young children continually ran in front of our jeeps to beg for money. One of them was run over and seriously injured. We had a doctor in the group, but the locals advised them not to do anything for fear of legal consequences if the child didn't survive.'

- 'I was shocked to see that some of the children had had their hands amputated. People told me that this was so that they could get more money from begging.'

- 'We were called in to plan an infrastructure project in a crisis region. The meeting was going well until we heard some explosions. We quickly moved into the bombproof "safe room". The next day I heard that several people had been killed in the bomb attack just a few hundred metres from our compound.'

Symptoms of culture shock range from a lack of energy and loss of appetite, to an inability to sleep or concentrate, hyperactivity and low self-confidence, to serious depression and, at the most extreme, thoughts of suicide. Oberg (1960) described the symptoms as follows:

> Some of the symptoms of culture shock are: excessive washing of the hands; excessive concern over drinking water, food dishes and bedding; fear of physical contact ...; the absent-minded, far-away stare (sometimes called 'the tropical stare'); a feeling of helplessness and a desire for dependence on long-term residents of one's own nationality; fits of anger over delays and other minor frustrations; delay and outright refusal to learn the language of the host country; excessive fear of being cheated, robbed, or injured; great concern over minor pains and irruptions of the skin; and finally, the terrible longing to be back home, to be able to have a good cup of coffee and a piece of apple pie, to walk into that corner drugstore, to visit one's relatives, and, in general, to talk to people who really make sense.

Phases of adjustment

There are several stages of acculturation or adaptation to foreign cultures. This often begins with a 'honeymoon' period when everything is interesting, exciting and new. Cultural fatigue follows when you get frustrated and annoyed as the realities of living in a different culture sink in and you start to miss things from home. You may face resistance from local employees who resent your privileged position. Young top talents who are sent to a country where age and seniority are respected may find it hard to get things done. If you are the only one in the team who doesn't speak the local language and this means that meetings have to be held in English, this can cause resentment, as the others are forced to expose their non-existent or inadequate language skills.

If your negative feelings are severe, or if your spouse or partner is unhappy, this can lead to a premature ending of the assignment. This is not only a difficult emotional decision for individuals but also a costly one for the company. An international delegation is expensive, and projects will suffer if the delegate has to be replaced.

Most people adjust to the new environment, even if they go through different phases of adjustment. Marx (1999) says that 'it is more realistic to use a model of culture shock that is not strictly linear but integrates a dynamic and repetitive cycle of positive and negative phrases until you break through culture shock'. It can be that your mood and satisfaction reach a new low point when you get deeper into the other culture and start seeing things below the surface you weren't initially aware of. This is often followed by a new, even higher, level of adaptation or 'fitting in'. You may have mixed feelings about going home, be unclear about what your future role will be in the company, and sad to leave new friends.

For some people 're-entry' or 'reverse culture shock' can be even more serious than the adjusting to life abroad. You may have had exciting responsibilities while away, and when you return home you find that people are not really interested in your experiences. It's a bit like showing someone your holiday photographs – they mean a lot to you but often not much to the person you are showing them to.

A more serious problem is that the company may struggle to find you a suitable position. The world has moved on without you. Although many experts talk about this, few companies invest enough time and energy in making sure that there is a smooth transition back for returning staff. This is a serious error as the reaction of some employees is to leave; the company not only loses a high-potential employee but also the knowledge they acquired while away.

These stages shown in Figure 11.1 are broadly similar to those in the change curve in Chapter 10 or to what people experience during depression or after the loss of a loved one. Everyone's experience is unique and the curve will inevitably vary for each individual.

Cultural adjustment curve

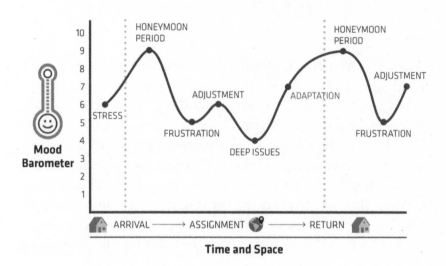

Figure 11.1 Cultural adjustment curve

Coping with transitions

Here are some ways of coping with these transitions:

Use the mood barometer

Have a mood barometer for you and your family to record how you are feeling. You can simply have smiley face Post-it notes which you stick onto the fridge door or wall and move up and down to reflect how satisfied you feel at the time. Your family members can do the same. If you are feeling down, then this simple method can send an important message to the other members of your family. Normally, the delegate, the partner and other family members find themselves at different stages of the cultural adjustment curve at different times.

Keep in touch

Through all phases it is important to keep in touch with family and trusted individuals at home. Make sure that you stay in contact with key stakeholders in the office in your home country. It is easy to be forgotten; 'out of sight' can easily mean 'out of mind'.

Network

As soon as you arrive, identify all the opportunities there are for building support networks; try to find local people who can support you. Get involved in leisure activities locally – this can be anything from joining a sports' team to singing in a choir or joining a book club. You may be able to get involved in tandem language learning: you and your counterpart learn each other's languages together. It can be helpful to connect with other expats and exchange experiences. This can, however, be negative if it ends up with simply meeting to complain about the host culture, like lonely colonists in the Raffles Hotel bar in Singapore at the time of the British Empire.

Beware of alcohol and drugs

The loneliness and depression which can be associated with international assignments can lead people to seek solace in alcohol and other drugs. Alcohol, in particular, may well be freely available – from the self-service bar in the business lounge at the airport to the minibar in the hotel, to the cocktails, aperitifs, sundowners and drinks receptions with your colleagues and clients. The bored expatriate spouse can easily be tempted to reach for the bottle to pass away the time at home. Keep an eye on your consumption and seek professional help if you suspect that you are in danger of becoming addicted. Problems with alcohol are more frequent than most people like to admit.

Support your partner

The dissatisfaction of the partner, or 'trailing spouse', is one of the most common reasons for the premature termination of international delegations. Partners need to be involved at every stage from the decision to accept the assignment to the re-entry process.

Many expat spouses and partners have interrupted their career to accompany the foreign assignee and find it difficult to find employment when away. They may not be able to get a work permit, and even if they do, their professional qualifications will not always be recognized. They may lack the language skills to work in a local company as well as a network which can help them find a job.

The important thing is for the partner to find meaningful activity. This can typically be getting involved in voluntary work or using the time to develop themselves through training and study.

Support your children

Many people find that children adapt easily to a new culture, and the experience of living abroad can be very exciting for them. That said, it is important that they are also involved in every stage. Talk about the move with them and try to get them interested in the destination that you are going to. One of the most important issues for them will be leaving their friends and having to settle into a new school. Think about sports and hobbies that they can get involved in.

More and more children can be described as third culture kids (TCKs). They have grown up in a culture other than that of their parents. They can often speak several languages but may lack a clear 'mother tongue'. They are often very skilled at adapting to new situations but can feel rootless. It can help them to know that they are not alone and that there are other children who are like this. They often form close relationships with other TCKs. Because they have experienced different perspectives, TCKs can be well suited to lead diverse teams.

Company support for foreign assignments

To maximize the effectiveness of the foreign assignment it is vital for companies to provide intercultural support for their delegates at every stage. The most important stages are shown in Figure 11.2.

Support for international assignments

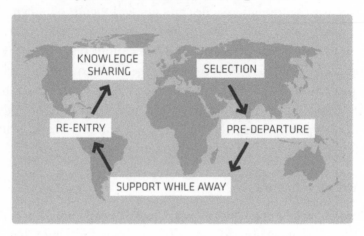

Figure 11.2 Support for international assignments

Selection

It all begins with the selection of who you want to send abroad. Restrict expensive long-term delegations to employees who you have identified as top talents and who can meet a strategic need in the target country. An example of this might be setting up a new sales office or production facility. Make sure the people you send have not only the business skills but also the intercultural skills needed to succeed. You can use an intercultural assessment tool (see Chapter 2); this should be combined with interviews and development centres involving representatives from the target culture.

Exploratory visits

Before the employee has to make a decision about whether to accept the delegation or not there should, if possible, be an opportunity for a 'look-and-see' trip to the destination. This is the exploratory visit.

Pre-departure training

Pre-departure training should prepare the employee for the cultural differences, making them aware of possible issues without unnecessarily increasing anxiety. It is vital that the spouse/partner and the children are also prepared in a way that is relevant to their roles. While many delegates request intercultural training for countries that they consider to be very different from their own, they often neglect to do this for cultures which they think they know or consider to be similar to their own. This can be a mistake. It is very different going to another country to live and work from going there on holiday, and the subtle differences between apparently close cultures can lead to serious problems if they are ignored.

Post-arrival training/coaching

Post-arrival training or coaching should be offered four to six weeks after work starts in the new location. By this time the delegate will have had some experience of the foreign culture. These experiences form the basis of the training. The role of the trainer or coach is to help the delegate to understand the cultural factors they have experienced and develop personal strategies to cope more effectively with them.

Social media platforms can be used to help delegates in a particular country to network and exchange useful information. Virtual 'expat cafés' provide help on everything from practical issues such as renting a flat or buying furniture from a previous delegate to meeting up for a meal. If the exchange involves sensitive information about customers and products, then it is essential that this is done behind a firewall with restricted access; there are plenty of horror stories of engineers posting requests for spare parts on publicly accessible social media platforms and thus unintentionally providing competitors with valuable information about a company's weak points.

Re-entry training

Before returning to their original country the employee should be given re-entry training in which they are encouraged to reflect on how they will cope with the transition and prepared for any new role. The 'home' organization also needs to be prepared for the returnee. Unfortunately, too many people leave companies after returning because this phase is neglected.

Knowledge sharing

The delegate has acquired highly valuable knowledge while away, and it is important that this is shared with the organization. This knowledge sharing is not just a question of politely looking at their photographs or filing a report but more of finding a way of capturing their unique experiences for the benefit of future delegates as well as the organization as a whole.

Going further

Marx, E. (1999) *Breaking through Culture Shock: What You Need to Succeed in International Business*, London: Nicholas Brealey.
Practical advice for coping with international assignments.
Pollock, D.C., Van Reken, R.E. and Pollock, M.V. (2010) *Third Culture Kids: The Experience of Growing Up Among Worlds*, 2nd edn, London: Nicholas Brealey.
The classic book about third culture kids.
Ward, C., Bochner, S. and Furnham, A. (2001) *The Psychology of Culture Shock*, 2nd edn. Hove: Routledge.
Exploration of the psychology behind contact with other cultures.
Weinberger, A. (2019) *The Global Mobility Workbook*, 3rd edn, Zurich: Global People Transitions.
A concise, practical guide for global mobility professionals.

12

Building Bridges

Strategies for Success

Beyond our ideas of right-doing and wrong-doing, there is a field, I'll meet you there.

Rumi

Key questions
- How can you cope effectively with cultural differences?
- How can you leverage differences for business success?

Exercise 12.1
Having read this book and reflected on your experiences of working in diverse global teams try to list ten key success factors. Compare your list with the keys to success described in this chapter.

The more you start seeing the complexity of dealing with diversity and cultural differences, the more overwhelming it can seem. This feeling can even become so daunting that you are unable to act at all. An HR manager from the Saudi Arabian office of an international company even requested that those on delegations to the region should not be given intercultural training, as they felt that many delegates were so worried about doing something wrong that they were simply paralysed and incapable of doing anything productive. It is not enough just to be sensitive to and understand differences; you also need to be able to deal with them effectively. This chapter looks at practical ways of coping with culture and turning differences into competitive advantage.

Ten keys to success

1 Be curious

Perhaps the best piece of advice about getting on with people from other cultures was given by the eighteenth-century German aristocrat Adolph Freiherr von Knigge. In his famous book *On Human Relations*, first published in 1788, he wrote 'Take an interest in others if you want others to take an interest in you.'

Have a genuine interest in finding out about other cultures, enjoy intercultural encounters and be keen to learn languages. Try to see cultural differences not as a problem to be tolerated but as something to be celebrated. Travel abroad doesn't automatically make you interculturally competent, but if you approach it with an open mind and curiosity it can contribute to developing your knowledge of different cultures.

A high-quality guide book is often a good start to finding information about other cultures. The Lonely Planet (www.lonelyplanet.com) or Rough Guides (www.roughguides.com) series provide well-researched and regularly updated practical information for travellers to many countries. Basic facts can also be found in the online *CIA World Factbook* (www.cia.gov/the-world-factbook/).

A great source of information is local 'informants': people who live in, or are from, the target culture. They don't necessarily have to be at the top of the hierarchy, but they need to be people you can trust and who understand their own as well as your culture. Experienced team assistants and interpreters can often be excellent informants as the nature of their work means that they are continually playing a mediator role.

2 Challenge stereotypes

As was shown in Chapter 5, if you try to apply the data on cultural dimensions to individual behaviour you are in danger of creating sophisticated stereotypes. While the results of the research by Hofstede and others can help us to understand tendencies, they cannot be used to predict individual behaviour. While lists of dos and don'ts seem attractive they can give a false sense of security. Culture is not like a machine, and, much as we might want it, there is no such thing as an operating manual.

3 Observe, don't judge

When travelling abroad take time to observe how people are behaving before you make a judgement or act. What is considered to be 'normal' will differ according to where you are and what the situation is. Observe how people dress, how they greet each other and how they behave during meetings. You don't have to copy what they do, but you will then have a better idea of what they might expect of you. If everyone is wearing casual clothing and you turn up in a formal suit you, and the others, will feel awkward. Don't immediately jump to conclusions about the behaviour of your business partners. If someone doesn't do something, or does it later than you expect, it doesn't necessarily mean that they are incompetent or lazy. Maybe they have a different attitude to time or simply have more important things to do. In fact, judging a person often tells you less about who they are and more about who you are.

Communicate effectively and in a culturally appropriate way. Rather than boasting about how much you know about a culture, pursue 'humble enquiry' based on open questions. Avoid controversial topics, like politics, when trying to make small talk. As one highly successful international project manager said: 'Ask, don't tell.'

4 Empathize

Empathy is the ability to see things from another person's perspective or 'put yourself in someone else's shoes'. Sometimes, of course, the shoes will be uncomfortable or won't fit at all. A better metaphor is putting on different cultural glasses and seeing things through another lens. Sometimes we need to add multiple lenses as when the optician tests your eyes for new glasses. Show respect for business partners from different cultures and try to understand their feelings and intentions. This doesn't mean that you have to agree with them, but at least try to understand where they person is coming from.

5 Switch codes

When we deal with other cultures we need to adapt. Caligiuri (2021) talks about 'cultural agility'. Molinsky (2013) uses the term 'global dexterity' to describe 'the capacity to adapt your behaviour in a new culture without losing yourself'. Having understood the culturally determined behaviour of your business partner, you may need to behave like a chameleon and change your behaviour according to the situation. Don't assume that methods that have been successful in your own culture will automatically work with people from others. To be successful you need to have a toolkit of techniques to deal with different types of people in different situations.

For instance, if you are working in a hierarchical culture but you are used to empowering your team to make their decisions, you will need to change your style. It will be necessary to 'switch codes'. Code-switching is adjusting your communication style and behaviour to those of the people around you.

Some people advocate a 'fake it until you make it' approach. This sometimes works but if you overdo it people will all too easily detect your lack of authenticity. This will, in turn, undermine trust. A Japanese proverb warns against this: 'The crow that imitates a cormorant drowns in the water.' Robbins (2021) shows how to combine code-switching with authenticity and resilience. Adapting too much is known as 'hypercorrection'. This means, for example, that the Western visitor has learned that the Japanese bow and exchange business cards and the Japanese has learned that Westerners shake hands. When they meet the Westerner wants to bow and the Japanese shake hands. Both are confused.

Take into account that most people will not expect 'foreigners' to behave exactly like they do, especially if you look different; sometimes 'creative misunderstandings' can actually lead to a better outcome than understanding. Generally, though, it is best not to overplay the 'foreigner card'. Just as with your frequent flyer card, at some point your bonus points run out.

Select the most effective option for the situation you are in. You can do this in several steps. The first step is to recognize that there is an issue and hear the 'cultural noise'. When you have done this and thought about the reasons for it, the next step is to be clear about what you are trying to achieve. Then you can decide which course of action is the best. You might decide to do nothing and simply accept the situation. Alternatives are to adapt to the other person, get the other to adapt to you or find a third way. For instance, if you are irritated by people using their phones in meetings, you can tolerate it, ask them to switch their phones off or request that they do their messaging in a break. Another solution would be to find a place where the signal is blocked.

6 Neither over- or underestimate the role of culture

As shown in Chapters 1 and 3, people are influenced by a number of cultural factors, only one of which is national culture. Each individual has multiple cultural identities. To work successfully with diverse groups, you need to understand the multicollectivity of your stakeholders. It is also important to remember that cultures are not static but are dynamic and interactive; the more cultures interact, the more they borrow from each other; this phenomenon is known as 'polyculturalism'.

7 Be mindful

The basis of our behaviour lies deep inside us. Mahatma Gandhi famously said: 'Your beliefs become your thoughts. Your thoughts become your words. Your words become your actions. Your actions become your habits. Your habits become your values. Your values become your destiny.' Our neural paths are formed in our childhood, but the brain is not fixed; it is constantly changing. Research is providing us with new insights into this 'neuroplasticity'.

We need to be aware of, and reflect critically on, our own culturally determined attitudes, beliefs and behaviour. The key to working successfully across cultures is not so much about understanding others but about understanding yourself: what are the triggers that annoy you or make you sad or happy? As Carl Jung said, 'Everything that irritates us about others can lead us to an understanding of ourselves.' Rosenberg (2015) echoed this when he pointed out that 'people may push your buttons, but they didn't install them'.

A useful model on self-awareness is the Johari house (Figure 12.1). The idea was developed by Handy (1993) on the basis of the Johari window by Luft (1969).

Johari house

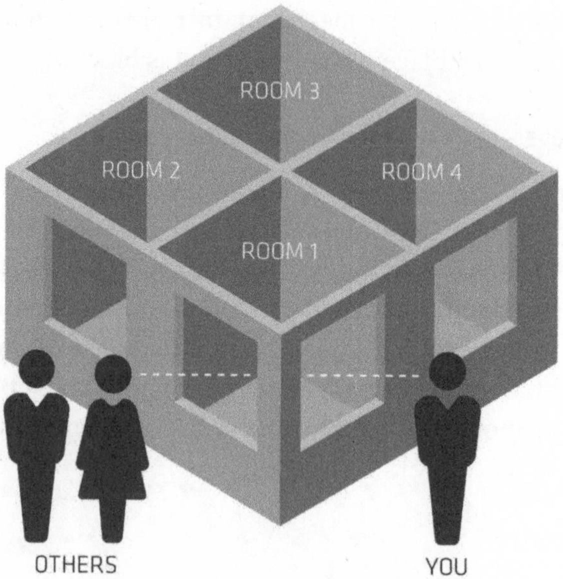

Figure 12.1 The Johari house

Room One is what both you and others see – the open self. Room Two contains the parts of you that only others see – the blind self.

Room Three cannot be seen by either you or others – the unknown self. Room Four is the part that you see but others can't – the private self. To become more self-aware and interculturally competent we need to make Room 1 larger. This happens through feedback from other and self-reflection.

It ultimately comes down to mindfulness: the ability to be fully present and aware of where you are and what you are doing. Mindfulness involves being aware of your body and how it reacts to different situations. In the intercultural context this means reflecting on the body's reaction when you come across something that is different. The Hakomi Method described by Kurtz (1990) is a powerful approach for exploring more deeply the connection between mind and body. Casey and Robinson (2017) suggest practical ways of 'consciously building the brain's capacity for inclusion'.

8 Celebrate difference

The US writer Audre Lorde, who described herself as a 'black, lesbian, feminist, warrior mother', said, 'It is not our differences that divide us. It is our inability to recognize, accept and celebrate those difference' (Lorde, 2007). Celebrate the diversity of your team. This does not have to be something abstract but can include tasting food or listening to music from the different cultures as part of team events. Ask team members to bring an item of food or drink from their country and have a potluck lunch or supper. Even try different dances, such as the waltz and the tango, as a way into exploring different cultures.

9 Bridge cultures

Cultural bridging involves recognizing differences and seeing how they can be connected to create synergies. Figure 12.2 shows an approach to bridging cultures which combines the mapping, bridging, integrating (MBI) model developed by DiStefano and Mazneski (2000) with the three-factor model of Barmeyer and Haupt (2007).

Bridging cultures

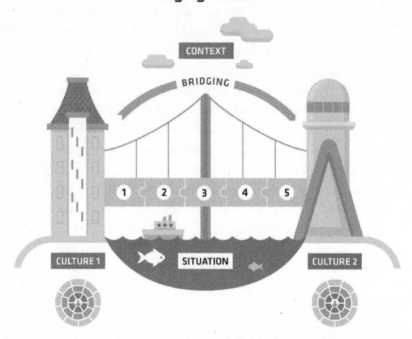

Figure 12.2 Bridging cultures

To understand what is happening and how to reach the best solution it is important to consider the general context or environment in which you are working, the situation you are in and the people and cultures involved. You can do this in five phases:

1. **Scan the context, situation and your culture.** The first step is to reflect on the culture of your team or organization against the background of the context and situation. As a basis for this, use relevant parts of the Wheel of Difference (see Chapter 3) and the Culture Navigation System (see Chapter 5). Try to identify the factors which have most influence, and exclude the factors that you can't change. Use a cultural assessment tool or seek help from an external consultant to provide an outside perspective.

2. **Scan the other culture.** The second step is to look carefully at the culture of the individuals, teams and organizations that

you are planning to collaborate with. You will never have access to all the information that you would like to have, but use as much as is available. This can include anything from looking at the company website and reading the annual report to checking the profiles of key stakeholders on social media. Do research to find out if there have been any significant recent developments in the company which have been reported in the media. If you are lucky enough to have a chance to visit the partners in their work environment, observe their interactions carefully to try to get an impression of what the company culture is really like. The reality may be quite different from what you found in the official literature.

3. **Identify differences and similarities.** At this phase it is important not only to focus on the differences but to see what the common ground is in terms of culture and interests. Identify possible targets for your collaboration and promising ways of working.

4. **Agree on common goals.** When you are ready to make an agreement make sure that all those involved have the same understanding of what you have agreed on. It is important to remember that what seems obvious to you may mean something quite different to someone from another culture. This stage will involve a great deal of clarifying and checking.

5. **Implement synergies.** At the implementation stage it is important that the dialogue continues and that you are constantly updating your culture scans. New differences can emerge but as you collaborate more intensively and get to know each other better you may well also discover new opportunities.

10 Never stop learning

The dream for some managers in international companies is of standardized training programmes which can be delivered globally online. The reality is somewhat different as it is clear that, as educational systems in different countries vary, so training has to be adapted to local conditions. Failure to do this will mean that training will be ineffective and waste precious resources.

In an open-space training session for an international company, participants worked in small groups on 'communication boards', completing tasks independent of the facilitator. A visiting Russian HR manager asked: 'Where is the teacher?' Coming from a teacher-centred educational background, he expected to see someone clearly instructing the participants, not just guiding them through the learning process. This doesn't mean to say that open-space activities cannot be used in Russia, but more effort may need to be made to explain them and persuade people of their effectiveness than may be the case where people have grown up with this sort of methodology.

Care has to be taken not to put people into cultural boxes. While preparing a Chinese–European team-building workshop in Shanghai some colleagues with experience of working there told the trainer that the Chinese educational system is based on rote learning and that they shouldn't use the sort of interactive games that are the centre of many team-building sessions in Europe and the USA. The trainer was cautious but decided to use them anyway. It turned out that the resistance to the games came exclusively from the European team members. 'Not another tower-building game,' they complained, while the Chinese team members tried to find out in advance what the next activity was going to be by asking questions like, 'What sort of shoes should I wear this afternoon?' and, 'Will we be going outside?' The fact was that the Europeans were, on average, much older than their Chinese counterparts and had simply got tired of this sort of activity, while the younger Chinese were excited by the novelty of the exercises.

Formal training

Corporate training is undergoing a radical transformation. Gone are the halcyon days of the lengthy residential country-specific intercultural briefings before a foreign assignment. The trend is also away from one-size-fits-all, function-general, country-specific to function-specific, culture-general intercultural training. In practice, this means that, instead of having a general workshop 'Working with the Arab World' open to all, you provide 'Intercultural Sensitivity for Senior Software Architects', customized for this specific function.

If you do invest in training think carefully about the provider you select. It is not enough just to have someone who has been to the country concerned or is from that country. This can be especially dangerous if the trainer's experience is not up to date. Gibson and Tang (2004) differentiate between various types of intercultural training. Classic **cultural briefings** focus on knowledge and dos and don'ts, and can take place with a large number of people, as there is little interaction. Their impact is limited and, at worst, they can spread unhelpful stereotypes.

Cultural assimilator training, which lends itself to e-learning, is based on analysis of critical incidents. While this can raise awareness, it can lead participants to thinking that there is one explanation for what is happening in a situation, rather than opening their eyes to the complexity of the Intercultural Cocktail (see Chapter 5).

Culture dimension training, which is highly suited to asynchronous online delivery, is based on the results of the research by Hofstede or Trompenaars or databases developed by the providers. It can help people become aware of their preferences but, as was shown in Chapter 5, can also lead to the propagation of stereotypes.

Beware, too, of **culture contrast training,** which is often based on the idea of two national cultures clashing and fails to take into account the multi-collectivity of the Wheel of Difference or multiple cultural identities (see Chapter 3), if it deals exclusively with national cultural standards.

Effective **intercultural business competence training** is based on a high level of interaction and authenticity. Case studies and critical incidents from the business area of the participants form the basis for role plays of situations, which are chosen for their relevance to the work of the participants. Face-to-face elements optimize use of time by focusing on experiential activities, while information is provided before and after the training on demand and online. Individuals can also be offered the training in the form of individual coaching.

Online training will be vital if you need to reach a large number of people or a group which is geographically dispersed. A **culture talk** can be used as a kick-off for a more widescale intervention. An expert on a country, region or topic is invited to give a presentation which is followed by questions and answers from the participants. The number of participants is limited only by the technical limits of the platform.

A more intensive and interactive version of this is the **culture clinic** in which a small group of six to eight participants bring their personal critical incidents to an online room, in which an expert facilitates a discussion and then provides analysis and makes recommendations. The **culture doctor** carries out a diagnosis and then prescribes a course of treatment.

Trainers that you use in any of these different forms of training need to have five main qualifications:

1. intercultural competence and knowledge

2. recent relevant business experience

3. training skills

4. language skills

5. professionalism.

The last of these is especially important, as the need for intercultural training is often connected with highly sensitive issues and confidentiality may be extremely important. Trainers should know their limits and not try to deal with issues outside their area of competence. For instance, if the client is being sent to a highly volatile region where there are security risks, then the behavioural training needs to be complemented with training from a security expert.

When medical issues play a role, for instance if someone returns from an assignment in a crisis zone with signs of post-traumatic stress disorder, specialist help is vital.

The intercultural toolkit

One way of approaching in-company intercultural learning is to integrate an intercultural toolkit into your learning ecosystem (Figure 12.4). Learning can be customized not only for the needs of each individual but also for the cultures in which the company is operating.

Intercultural Toolkit

BEST PRACTICE

REPORTS

TESTS

COUNTRY PROFILES

TRAINING

RESOURCES

Figure 12.3 The intercultural toolkit

The intercultural toolkit can include the following:

- **Country profiles.** Culture-specific information and links to information about the different countries that you are working with.

- **Training providers.** Contact details and reviews of tried-and-tested providers of intercultural and language training and coaching, either online or in your area.

- **Best practice.** A collection of reports on international projects which have been successful. It can also help to have examples of worst practices so that mistakes are not repeated.

- **Resources.** Articles, videos and training materials which have proved useful.

- **Tests.** Access to selected intercultural competence assessment tests.

- **Reports.** Reports from project teams and delegates returning from foreign assignments.

The learning diary

Developing intercultural competence is part of a lifelong journey based on experience, learning and, above all, reflection. In addition to setting up an intercultural toolkit for your team keep your own learning diary in which you record and reflect on your cultural moments (Figure 12.4). This is an example of what a diary could look like. It is based on the OAR approach described in the Introduction.

Situation: When? Where? Who?	01.03. Virtual meeting. All team members.
Observations: What happened?	X didn't contribute any ideas to the budget discussion. Other team members seemed surprised.
Analysis: Why did it happen?	Technical problems? Topic too sensitive? Communication style: turn-taking? Power distance? Introvert v. extrovert?
Recommendations: What can be done?	Arrange one-to-one call with X to learn what happened and get X's ideas. Adapt future meeting style if needed to make it more inclusive.

Figure 12.4 The learning diary

Most people realize how important it is to devote time to physical fitness; to be successful in the VUCA world, you also need to train yourself to be open-minded and ultimately build bridges across cultural divides.

Going further

Adler, N.J. and Gundersen, A. (2008) *International Dimensions of Organizational Behavior*, 5th edn, Mason, OH: Thomson South-Western.
An overview of the influence of culture on a wide range of different aspects of organizations.
Barmeyer, C. and Franklin, P. (eds) (2016) *Intercultural Management: A Case-Based Approach to Achieving Complementarity and Synergy*, London: Palgrave Macmillan.
An analysis of real-life case studies with the stress on finding positive outcomes and synergies; especially suitable for use on MBA courses.
The CIA World Factbook is a source of regularly updated country-specific information: www.cia.gov/the-world-factbook/
CIT4VET – Open Online Catalogue of Intercultural Tools for Vocational Education and Training is a free online catalogue which provides links to a range of intercultural tools for use with culturally diverse groups: https://cit4vet.erasmus.site/open-online-catalogue/
The Society for Intercultural Education, Training and Research (SIETAR) is the world's largest international, interdisciplinary network of interculturalists. It has national and regional organizations throughout the world which publish journals and newsletters and organize conferences and workshops: www.sietareu.org/national-sietars/

Answer key

Chapter 1

Exercise 1.1

1. Especially at higher levels of management an international business culture is emerging: international airports and shopping malls have a certain similarity about them. When you go deeper you will often find significant differences in how people think and act. The fact that people are more mobile than ever before and exposed to many different cultural influences makes it hard to put them into 'cultural boxes'. **See Chapter 1.**

2. The fact that your company has been successful in the past doesn't mean that it will necessarily be successful in the future. Travel can provide you with experience but it is not the same as intercultural competence. **See Chapter 2.**

3. Monocultural teams are likely to either under- or overperform when compared to multicultural teams. A great deal depends on how suitable the members of the team are and how well they are led. For some tasks it may be an advantage to have a monocultural team. However, if, for instance, it is important to be innovative, then a multicultural team is necessary to provide different perspectives. **See Chapters 3, 7 and 8.**

4. We all have mental filters or biases. While it is possible to become aware of your personal biases and take steps to

mitigate the negative effects of bias in teams and organizations, it is not possible to get rid of bias completely. **See Chapter 4.**

5. Of course, it is good to have quantitative data but beware of reducing culture to a few dimensions. China is supposed to be collectivist but how far can we really generalize about 1.4 billion people? **See Chapter 5.**

6. As English is the *lingua franca* of international business you obviously have an advantage, but it is worth checking whether others feel the same about your English as you do. You may be unpleasantly surprised. **See Chapter 6.**

7. It depends on what the purpose of the meeting is. If you are getting to know team members at the beginning of a project, a face-to-face meeting can be very useful. But for routine meetings virtual communication can be more flexible, cheaper and more efficient. **See Chapter 7.**

8. This is easier said than done. Whether team members will come and see you will also depend on their understanding of your role as a manager. **See Chapter 8.**

9. How people gain the respect and trust of others also differs widely across cultures. It is not always as a result of competence or expertise. **See Chapter 9.**

10. This can be an important step but much more is needed if the desired change is really going to spread throughout the organization. **See Chapter 10.**

11. Travelling on short trips for leisure is quite different from living and working in a country for a longer time. **See Chapter 11.**

12. Although most people try to adapt their behaviour to the environment in which they are, it is hard to change deep-seated habits quickly. There are other ways of dealing with difference. See **Chapter 12.**

Chapter 2

Exercise 2.2

These are some examples of behaviour shown by people who are interculturally competent. The higher your score the better.

Exercise 2.3

1. There are many different types of greeting in different countries around the world. Examples are shaking hands, kissing on the cheek or hand, hugging, bowing and handing over a business card. The greetings vary not only according to the country but the relationship you have with the person you are greeting and the situation you are in.

2. There are again many variations. Examples are fast food, sandwiches, snacks in a home office, visits to the canteen, meals in a café or restaurant, shared meals with the group, cheese rolls and glasses of milk.

3. Even in the same company dress codes can vary according to the situation. Here are some real-life examples found within one international corporation:

   - suits without ties (HQ in Germany)
   - suits with ties (Finance Department, Monday–Thursday)
   - casualwear (Finance Department, Friday)
   - sportswear (Finance Department, team-building day)
   - jeans and socks but no shoes (software developers)
   - full-length white robe (regional HQ in Dubai).

Exercise 2.4

1. No risk. No fun.
+ entrepreneurial spirit; – carelessness

2. There's no time for small talk.
+ focused; – cold

3. Time is money.
+ urgency; – impatient

4. When the going gets tough, the tough get going.
+ competitive; – aggressive

5. It was just a joke.
+ entertaining; – not serious

6. Do your own thing.
+ individual freedom; – selfish

7. Every cloud has a silver lining.
+ optimistic; – unrealistic

8. What's your bottom line?
+ clarity; – impatient

Case: The battery factory – Exercise 2.5

Country A = China; Country B = Germany

The dramatic development of the Chinese economy since the 1990s means that more Chinese companies are investing in other countries than ever before; this trend is likely to continue. In this case, several factors need to be considered if the investment is to be successful. Chinese and local managers will need to consider their management style. A style which is accepted and effective in China will not necessarily work in Europe. This will include knowledge of work regulations. The common practice in technology companies in China of working 9–9–6 (9.00a.m.–9.00p.m. six days a week) will not be acceptable in most situations in European countries – it may even be illegal.

Careful consideration should be given to recruiting. What is the employment situation for skilled workers in the region or country? How can the best employees be found and hired? What will be needed to retain key staff? How will teams cope with different languages?

The influx of such a large number of foreigners into a small town will also have to be considered carefully. Is suitable accommodation available? What is the attitude of the local population to them coming in? What will be done to help Chinese employees and their families settle into life abroad? How can the local employees be prepared for working in an international team?

Chapter 4

Exercise 4.1

This is an optical illusion. Although they may look different, the tables both have the same length and width.

Exercise 4.2

This story, known as the 'Surgeon's Dilemma', is often used to demonstrate the way that unconscious bias works. The surgeon is the boy's mother.

Chapter 5

Critical incident: Missing the flight – Exercise 5.1

Country A = USA; Country B = Germany

This is an example of *person versus task orientation*. In cultures which tend to be task-oriented the priority is getting the task done; in person-oriented cultures it is essential to foster the relationship before getting down to the task. The German airline official in this example no doubt felt that the most important thing was to get all queuing passengers their new tickets as quickly as possible and not 'waste time' with 'unnecessary' small talk; the American, missing an apology or explanation, interpreted this as 'unfriendliness' and 'terrible service'.

Cultures which tend to be more person-oriented than task-oriented will spend a considerable time building up a relationship before they get down to business. US and European businesspeople doing business with Arab countries are often frustrated at the time it takes to get down to business, wondering why they are being entertained and asked about their private life. In many cultures it is essential to know the person you are dealing with before you can do the deal; once the trust is there, the business can go surprisingly quickly.

Critical incident: Phones in meetings – Exercise 5.2

This illustrates a difference in attitude to *time*. Those who are using their phones and other devices in the meetings may not be interested in the meeting but may also be from *polychronic* cultures in which multitasking is acceptable. Those who want phones to be switched off demonstrate behaviour found in *monochronic* cultures.

The manager may decide that it is acceptable for people to behave like this. Otherwise they may need to get the group to agree to rules for meetings or, especially if they are dealing with people from a high power distance culture, just use their power as a manager and tell the team how meetings are going to be run.

Critical incident: How many parts? – Exercise 5.3

Country A = UK; Country B = Germany

This is an example of different attitudes to planning and *uncertainty avoidance*. The British, in this case, think that planning is important but that the plan can and should be changed as the circumstances change; they are focused more on the result than the process. For the German team, which has higher uncertainty avoidance, once the plan has been agreed it should be kept to unless there is a new decision; they will put considerable effort into the plan and don't expect it to be changed without good reason. If there needs to be a change, they would expect there to be another meeting during which the change request can be approved.

Critical incident: Congratulations – Exercise 5.4

Country A = UK; Country B = Japan

This is an example of *individualism* versus *collectivism*. In individual cultures it is normal to single out and praise the contribution of an individual in front of the group while in collectivist cultures this is not done, as the group achievement is the most important thing. The Japanese have a saying, 'The nail that sticks out gets hammered down.' In a meeting it is not good for the manager to single out one member of the team either for criticism or praise.

Critical incident: The retreat – Exercise 5.5

Country A = Germany; Country B = China

Differences in attitudes to *power distance* and the display of status are at the heart of this case. The Chinese delegation, far from appreciating the informal style of the management centre, interpreted it as a lack of respect that they were staying in such simple accommodation and that everyone was treated as being on the same hierarchical level. As far as the dinner invitation was concerned, the Chinese customers were expecting to be entertained not only by the management team but by the CEO.

The organizer in fact saved the situation by telling the driver to take the Chinese to wherever they wanted to go while she hastily arranged a breakfast meeting the next day with the CEO. Even though the Chinese delegates had only a brief discussion with him, the fact that he had found time for them was enough to convince them that they were being respected and that they should sign the contract.

Critical incident: Slot reservation – Exercise 5.6

Country A = United Arab Emirates; Europe = B

This illustrates different *attitudes to rules*. While for the Europeans it was a normal part of the business process to require reservation fees, the Arab customer was disturbed by having to sign the agreements every few months. Each renewal meant that he had to go to his superior for a signature, something which was humiliating for him. He even described the renewals as 'documented mistrust'. The key to keeping the Arab customer would have been to invest much more time looking after the relationship rather than alienating him by strict adherence to formal procedures.

Chapter 6

Critical incident: Checking-in – Exercise 6.2

Country A = Germany; Country B = USA

This illustrates two attitudes to planning and decision-making. The German colleague understood that the US colleague would deliver the figures on time as agreed. The US colleague had agreed, but as they had not heard anything from their German counterpart they assumed that the figures were no longer a priority; they expected some more communication or 'checking-in'.

Exercise 6.3

1. **Starting with a joke.** Humour can help to create a good atmosphere but, especially in international settings, has to be used with care. Many jokes are based on cultural stereotypes, which can cause offence.

2. **Reading a written text.** This can give you a sense of security, particularly if you are speaking in a foreign language, and may be necessary for highly technical presentations. On the other hand, it may make your presentation feel stiff and will reduce eye contact with the audience.

3. **Involving the audience.** People from some cultures welcome interaction between the audience and the speaker. In other cultures it can be considered disrespectful to interrupt the speaker. The best thing to do is to make clear at the beginning of the presentation how you wish to proceed.

4. **Keeping to the time limit.** People from monochronic cultures will welcome strict adherence to the time schedule, while in polychronic cultures it can be considered impolite to stop someone from speaking because of the time limit. A French participant at an international meeting who was asked to stop after they had exceeded the time limit said to the facilitator: 'What is more important, your clock or my ideas?'

5. **Making the structure very clear.** People from monochronic or linear cultures with high uncertainty avoidance will feel reassured by knowing what is happening. People from more relationship-oriented, polychronic cultures may find this too rigid and feel that it doesn't allow enough room for spontaneity.

6. **Providing the audience with handouts.** This may distract the audience from your presentation or may be appreciated if the participants need visual support.

7. **Dressing formally.** Match the way you dress to the event. If in doubt, ask the organizers beforehand what is appropriate.

8. **Looking serious.** This depends very much on the topic and the situation as well as the cultural background of the audience.

9. **Only taking questions at the end of the presentation.** Clarify this with the audience before you start.

10. **Using slides and other visual aids.** Slides can reinforce your argument, but if you use too many then there is a danger of 'death by PowerPoint'.

11. **Summarizing what you have said at the end of the presentation.** This can be a useful way of reinforcing your argument, but for some it might seem a dull and predictable way of ending.

12. **Telling anecdotes.** People from many cultures appreciate story-telling and personal anecdotes. Whether you use them or not will depend on the topic as well as the audience.

Critical incident: Be prepared – Exercise 6.4

Country A = USA; Country B = Germany

The problem here is that the two sides have different expectations of what the meeting is about. The American expects a brainstorming-type session in which the group works together to reach a decision; the Germans expect to work ahead of the meeting preparing possible solutions which can be the basis for a decision in the meeting. The key to resolving this is to make the expectations explicit and agree on a common understanding on what the meetings are about and what sort of preparation is expected.

Critical incident: The budget meeting – Exercise 6.5

A is from Germany; B is from the UK

A was trying to reduce the tension by relaxing his posture, and using humour to improve the atmosphere. B interpreted this as their not taking the conversation seriously.

Critical incident: Leadership training – Exercise 6.6

Country A = Greece; Country B = USA; Country C = UK

Pitch, intonation and volume of voice differ widely across cultures. Because they were unaware of this, the trainers assumed that Greek is like English and interpreted the exchanges as aggressive when for the Greek participants they were normal.

Exercise 6.7

The first thing to clarify is what the aim of the meeting is. If it is exclusively to provide information, then think carefully about whether you really need a face-to-face meeting or whether it could be done virtually. If, as is often the case, the aim is to combine providing information with networking and motivating the team, then the agenda needs to be changed. The present draft doesn't leave nearly enough space for this; there needs to be much more time for interaction. Having the meeting at the production facility means that there is a tangible link to the business, but it can also mean distractions for people who work at the site. Sometimes it is better to choose a convenient location away from the immediate workplace.

At first sight the agenda looks well structured. Points that need to be thought about include the starting and finishing times of the meeting. The 8.30am start might be too early for those travelling in on the day. No time is included for introducing the participants or for breaks. The question-and-answer session is a good idea, but it too has to be managed carefully. An alternative to having an open discussion is to provide participants with cards on which they write questions, collecting them in and clustering them into topic groups. The facilitator can then pose the questions to the panel. Software is available to do this digitally. Participants use their phone to write comments or questions, which are then sent to a tablet used by the facilitator. This can be combined with brain-storming activities and polls to activate the audience.

These methods prevent one or two people from dominating the discussion and, by making the person who asked the question anonymous, allow people to raise controversial issues without being exposed in front of the group; for introverts or people from cultures in which it is considered to be impolite to criticize people in public this may be especially important. It does, however, require openness from the speakers and needs to be agreed with them before the meeting. It may not be appropriate in high power distance cultures.

Some participants will feel that the lunch break is too short; it should be made longer to allow time for informal exchanges. The idea of placing the factory tour after lunch is good as a way of overcoming the danger of having a 'graveyard slot' after lunch. Allow enough time to get to the factory and for safety procedures and putting on protective clothing before the tour.

The afternoon is packed with presentations with little room for discussion. A way of loosening this up would be to replace the product presentations with an interactive 'marketplace' in which those responsible have stands with information while the participants circulate around the room talking to them. This will also provide participants with a chance to network.

It would be a good idea to give the group a break between the closing speech and the departure for dinner so that they can catch up on calls, get ready and have some more informal contact time. For some cultures the beginning and end of the dinner will be too early. While, of course, many participants will want to try local food, it is very important that the dietary requirements of the group are taken in to consideration.

Chapter 7

Exercise 7.1

This style of meeting is not universally applicable. It may work for you and your team but it may not be suitable in some situations for some people from some cultures. It reflects a *monochronic* and linear approach to time – one thing is done after the other. It is an example of *low-context* communication where messages have to be explicit. It shows *high uncertainty avoidance*, indicated by the emphasis on planning. Structure and rules, rather than flexibility and spontaneity, are important. At the beginning and end the participants are expected to share their feelings – not everyone will necessarily feel comfortable doing this. While having the camera on may be fine for many people, for others it may be intimidating and intrusive.

A Chinese colleague looking at this commented that in China many business meetings are often much more spontaneous than this and would often take place on mobile phones on the go without warning, without using the picture function and while multitasking. The focus is on connecting people as quickly and frequently as possible rather than structure and planning. A joke is that Chinese meetings are better than Western ones because in China you can use your phone while eating with chopsticks, while a Westerner can't when using a knife and fork.

There is no universally perfect way of running virtual meetings. It is clear that frequent high-quality communication is a key ingredient. Use all available channels in a way that suits as many of the team members as possible, for the tasks in hand, in the situation that you are in.

Critical incident: Silence is golden – Exercise 7.3

Country A = UK; Country B = Sweden

A key to understanding this situation is to be aware that different cultures have different attitudes to turn-taking. In this case the Swedish manager was patiently waiting for a chance to make a comment while their British colleagues were so engrossed in their debate that they left very little space for their Swedish counterparts. Fortunately, the chairperson was sensitive to this, reacted to the non-verbal signals indicated by the intense concentration on the conversation, and brought the Swedish colleagues into the discussion. By doing this they paved the way for a solution to the problem. Attitudes to turn-taking similar to those of the Swedes can be observed in meetings with participants from Japan and China.

Chapter 8

Case: The project team – Exercise 8.2

Running international teams under pressure to achieve results in a short time is challenging. There is no easy answer to the problems described here. One key to understanding what is happening is to think clearly about how the team members from the different countries see their roles within the team and what they expect from you as the project manager. This will differ in the different phases. When arranging the virtual meetings, remember to take time zones into account.

Case: The business plan – Exercise 8.3

Country A = UK; Country B = Germany

The two people from different countries see the role of the manager differently and communicate in different ways. B expects the manager to give clear instructions, while A prefers a more delegative style with the employee taking on responsibility for deciding on priorities. A's communication is more high context and indirect then B's.

The business plan

What A said/did	What B said/did	What A thinks	What B thinks
'I have heard that you have a lot of experience with supporting customers who come to us from other countries. If you have a moment then it would be great if you could put together your ideas for me.'		I've asked her to prepare a business plan for supporting international customers.	He's asking me to think about the topic if I have time. It is not a priority.
	'That's true. Fine – I'd be happy to do that.'	She has promised to deliver.	I'll do it if I have time.
	B didn't have much to do and so prepared some slides on the topic. The next morning she sends them to A.	She will work on the presentation.	By chance I happened to have some time.
'Thanks a lot – that's just what I need for the management meeting this afternoon. This could be a key part of our business plan for next year.'		Great – she has done what I asked her to do.	Lucky I did it – I didn't realize it was so urgent.

	'I didn't realize that it was so urgent. You should have told me.'	Strange. Wasn't it clear to her that it was urgent?	Why didn't he tell me he needed it for the management meeting?
'I thought my instructions were quite clear.'		I gave clear instructions.	Strange. He didn't give me any sense of urgency.

Case: The matrix – Exercise 8.4

It is important to bear in mind that structures which work well in one place may not work at all in others. The matrix structures in which people work on a project for a project manager who is not their disciplinary manager are hard to manage in high power distance cultures. In these cultures, the employee may well only look to their line manager for instructions and ignore those coming from the project manager. In these cases, the project manager will have to look at other ways of influencing without formal authority.

Case: The binational team – Exercise 8.5

Country A = Germany; Country B = China

Analysis

Here are some of the cultural factors which play a role in this case. The analysis refers to this specific situation and is not meant to suggest that all German – Chinese teams work like this.

Responsibility. While the German members of this team think that the Chinese don't take enough responsibility, the Chinese don't feel they are given any. The two sides have a different idea of what taking responsibility means. While for the Germans it means acting independently within a predefined framework, the Chinese find it too tight and want to be able to influence strategy and targets as well as processes. They are pragmatic and ignore or circumvent procedures if they feel this is necessary to achieve their goals.

Decision-making. The Chinese team members expect their managers to make clear decisions – this, according to the Chinese, is what they are paid for. The Germans believe that decisions can be delegated.

Meetings. The Chinese side don't see the importance of the meetings and therefore are late or don't turn up at all. They want to communicate with their managers but not with the whole team. Coming from a high power distance culture they think that if the managers are not present at the meetings then there is little point in attending.

Direct communication style. The German style of direct communication is alien to the Chinese group. They do give feedback but in a different way from the Germans. Rather than stating it explicitly, they indicate disapproval by avoiding the problem, staying silent or failing to cooperate.

Educational background. In this case the young Chinese engineers have an excellent theoretical knowledge but lack the practical experience of their Western partners. The job profiles do not match those that the Germans are used to.

Work versus private life. The Chinese do not distinguish as sharply between work and private life as the Germans do. They are expected to have their phones on at all times. If the boss calls a meeting at the weekend, even if this is at short notice, they will be expected to go.

In judging whether they can trust their foreign manager, the Chinese will look at the whole person and this includes behaviour outside of the workplace. The time difference of six to seven hours between China and Germany also makes it difficult to communicate during normal office hours.

Loyalty. In a situation where foreign companies are competing for labour in China, the locals can play off companies against each other. This is not regarded as unethical but merely as a pragmatic loyalty to the market rather than loyalty to one particular company.

Recommendations

- As in all international teams, the leader has to invest time in clarifying expectations of team members and getting agreement on how everyone wants to work together.

- The two sides need to agree on which processes are absolutely necessary and which are 'nice to have'; some flexibility on both sides is desirable.

- The two sides need to become aware that there are different management styles and agree on an appropriate style for the whole team.

- The German side has to communicate clearly the importance of the meetings and ensure that all who are needed attend the meetings to ensure that decisions can be made.

- A prerequisite for effective feedback is trust between the parties – some time needs to be spent on relationship building and establishing rules for feedback which respect the sensitivities of both sides.

- Western companies recruiting Chinese staff would be well advised to seek local advice on what exactly the applicants' qualifications mean.

- The German side needs to make sure they appoint someone to stand in for them when they are out of office and their contact details need to be communicated to their Chinese colleagues.

Chapter 9

Case: Global data – Exercise 9.1

This is a very common problem. Without even needing to look at country specifics, it is worth thinking about the following factors if you are faced with this sort of situation. The first thing to look at is the relationship between HQ and the regions: do the structures and incentives encourage or hinder cooperation? The fact that the figures aren't delivered or are not of the quality required suggests that there might be something wrong here.

Think about your communication style. Are you relying too heavily on the fact that people must do something because it is in their job description, or are you communicating clearly the reasons why the information is important for overall business success and the benefits of providing that information? The benefit arguments can be especially important in cultures where people are driven by: 'What's in it for me?'

The Global Sales Manager needs to think about their personal relationship with the partners in the regions. In many cultures, good personal relationships and a high level of rapport are essential before you can get down to business.

Case: The negotiation – Exercise 9.2

A = Europe; Country B = India

Analysis

In some cultures, people will want a rough estimate of price before they start negotiating. They realize that the price may not be precise and may change, but think that there is no point in getting into details if it is completely out of scope. In other cultures, detailed analysis of requirements is necessary before a price is named; this is often found in high uncertainty avoidance cultures. The comment 'Yes, that's fine' misleads the salesperson. It does not necessarily indicate agreement but more a desire to keep harmony and avoid 'loss of face'; this is an example of high-context communication.

Recommendations

It is important to be aware that negotiating styles differ in different cultures. To be successful you may need to alter your style; in this case it would be a good idea to give a rough estimate before you make a formal offer. When dealing with cultures where communication tends to be indirect or high context, you will need to ask additional questions to find out what a phrase like 'Yes, that's fine' really means.

Critical incident: The window – Exercise 9.4

The model of conflict resolution can be used to illustrate the options in this case. The 0/0 position would be if they are moved into different offices. The 0/10 and 10/0 positions are when the window is either open or closed the whole time. The 5/5 position would be if the window is partly open, or open for part of the time. The win-win position is if they can find a way of airing the room without causing a draught, such as by opening a window in an adjacent office or using a ventilator fan.

Where there is air conditioning in the office, then the situation can become even more complicated. The temperature which is comfortable for people depends on what they are used to. The individuals in an office may not be able to control the thermostat if it is centrally controlled for technical or energy-saving reasons. If you have a visitor from a temperate climate, where air conditioning is not so common, then it is helpful to warn them that, although the outside temperature may by over 30° C, the room temperature will be much cooler. For their comfort, they may want to bring some warmer clothes with them to wear in the office or meeting room.

Chapter 10

Case: The global HR process – Exercise 10.1

Apart from the usual resistance to a new process, a number of cultural issues emerged during the rollout. Although the idea of setting targets was widely accepted, some managers from collectivist cultures wanted there to be group rather than individual targets.

Some managers felt that the monitoring phase was not necessary as either they had constant contact with their employees or they felt that the employees should be left alone to work independently and judged on the results at the end of the year. This reflected culturally determined differences in management styles.

Some people in countries with high inflation felt that the pay round should be more frequent than once a year.

There were different attitudes to how the round table should work. While those from consensus-oriented cultures accepted that the measures should be the result of decisions by the whole management team, managers in some high power distance countries felt that each manager should make up their own mind about how much the pay increase should be and that this decision should not be transparent to the other members of the management team.

Case: Close neighbours – Exercise 10.2

Country A = Germany; Country B = Austria

What at first sight seems to be a trivial case reveals, on closer examination, some fundamentally different attitudes to communication in the workplace. The German managers were used to working in a large organization in which communication had to be highly formalized. The Austrians, on the other hand, belonged to a smaller company in which the boss spent much more time in informal contact with the employees. They were used to informal contact over a cup of coffee and regular visits after work to the café or *Heuriger*, or wine tavern. Alongside the different sizes of the companies, national cultural differences also play a role: there is a contrast between the task orientation of the German management and the higher degree of relationship orientation of the Austrian staff.

For the cooperation to be more successful both sides have to try to understand the other better. The Austrians need to appreciate that the German managers are simply used to a different way of working and that they are not intending to send negative signals to the Austrian workforce. The managers, for their part, may find that a bit more time invested in building relationships will pay off in the long run.

References

Adesina, Z. and Marocico, O. (2017) Is it easier to get a job if you're Adam or Mohamed? *BBC Inside Out*, 6 February. Retrieved from www.bbc.com/news/uk-england-london-38751307

Adler, N.J. and Gundersen, A. (2008) *International Dimensions of Organizational Behavior*, 5th edn, Mason, OH: Thomson South-Western.

Bach, M. (n.d.) www.innovatingcanada.ca/diversity/diversity-is-a-fact-inclusion-is-a-choice/

Banaji, M.R. and Greenwald, A.G. (2013) *Blindspot: Hidden Biases of Good People*, New York: Delacorte.

Barmeyer, C. and Haupt, U. (2007). Interkulturelles Coaching, in J. Straub, A. Weidemann and D. Weidemann (eds), Handbuch interkulturelle Kommunikation und Kompetenz. Grundbegriffe – Theorien – Anwendungsfelder, Stuttgart: Metzler, 784–93.

Barmeyer, C. and Franklin, P. (eds) (2016) Intercultural Management: A Case-Based Approach to Achieving Complementarity and Synergy, London: Palgrave Macmillan.

Bauer, J. (2008) Prinzip Menschlichkeit. Warum wir von Natur aus kooperieren, Munich: Wilhelm Heyne Verlag.

Bennett, M.J. (1993) Towards Ethnorelativism: A Developmental Model of Intercultural Sensitivity, in R.M. Paige (ed), Education for the Intercultural Experience, 2nd edn, Yarmouth: Intercultural Press, 21–71.

Boeijen, A. van and Zijlstra, Y. (2020) Culture Sensitive Design: A Guide to Culture in Practice, Amsterdam: BIS Publishers.

Bolten, J. (2018) Einführung in die Interkulturelle Wirtschaftskommunikation, 3rd edn, Göttingen: Vandenhoeck & Ruprecht.

Bourke, J. (2016) The six signature traits of inclusive leadership: Thriving in a diverse new world, *Deloitte Insights*, 14 April. Retrieved from www2.deloitte.com/us/en/insights/topics/talent/six-signature-traits-of-inclusive-leadership.html

Brake, T. (2008) *Where in the World is My Team? Making a Success of Your Virtual Global Workplace*, Chichester: Wiley & Sons.

Bryce, E. (2020) What's the difference between race and ethnicity? *livescience.com*, 8 February. Retrieved from www.livescience.com/difference-between-race-ethnicity.html

Brinkmann, U. and Van Weerdenburg, O. (2014) *Intercultural Readiness*, Houndmills: Palgrave Macmillan.

Caligiuri, P. (2021) *Build Your Cultural Agility: The Nine Competencies of Successful Global Professionals*, London: Kogan Page.

Casey, M.E. and Murphy Robinson, S. (2017) *Neuroscience of Inclusion: New Skills for New Times*, Outskirts Press.

Catalyst (2014) *Diversity Matters, New York: Catalyst*. Retrieved from www.catalyst.org/research/infographic-diversity-matters/

Charta der Vielfalt, https://www.charta-der-vielfalt.de/en/understanding-diversity/diversity-management/

Comfort, J. and Franklin, P. (2014) *The Mindful International Manager: How to Work Effectively Across Cultures*, 2nd edn, London: Kogan Page.

Deardorff, D.K. (ed.) (2009) *The SAGE Handbook of Intercultural Competence*, Thousand Oaks, CA: SAGE.

De Bono, E. (2016) *Six Thinking Hats: Run Better Meetings, Make Faster Decisions*, London: Penguin Life.

Dignen, B. and McMaster, I. (2013) *Communication for International Business*, London: Collins.

DiStefano, J.J. and Maznevski, M.L. (2000) Creating value with diverse teams in global management, *Organizational Dynamics*, 29(1): 45–63.

DiStefano, L., Imon, S., Lee, H. and DiStefano, J. (2005) Bridging differences: a model for effective communication between different disciplines through training programmes for professionals, *City & Time*, 1(2).

Earley, P.C. and Ang, S. (2003). *Cultural Intelligence: Individual Interactions Across Cultures*, Stanford, CA: Stanford University Press.

Eisenberger, N.I. (2012) The neural bases of social pain, *Psychosomatic Medicine*, February/March, 74(2), 126–35.

Elger, K. (2020) The concept of race is taboo, *Der Spiegel*, 25/20, 16 June.

Fisher, R. and Brown, S. (1989) *Getting Together: Building Relationships As We Negotiate*, New York: Penguin.

References

Fleming, S.M., Thomas, C.L. and Dolan, R.J. (2010) Overcoming status quo bias in the human brain, *Proceedings of the National Academy of Sciences*, March, 107(13): 6005–9.

Furnham, A. and Petrova E. (2010) *Body Language in Business*, Houndmills: Palgrave Macmillan.

Gardenswartz, L. and Rowe, A. (2003) *Diverse Teams at Work: Capitalizing on the Power of Diversity*, Alexandria, VA: Society for Human Resource Management.

Gibson, R. (2002) *Intercultural Business Communication*, Oxford: Oxford University Press.

Gibson, R., Tauber, T. and Münster, M. (2003) Return on Culture: Interkulturelle Kompetenzentwicklung für das internationale Geschäft, *Wirtschaftspsychologie aktuell*, 2: 12–15.

Gibson, R. and Tang, Z. (2004) Aufbau interkultureller Geschäftskompetenz, in L. von Rosenstiel, L. et al. (eds), *Strategisches Kompetenzmanagement*, Wiesbaden: Gabler Verlag, 237–50.

Glasl, F. (1999) *Confronting Conflict. A first-aid kit for handling conflict*, Stroud: Hawthorne Press.

Goleman, D. (1995) *Emotional Intelligence: Why It Can Matter More than IQ*, New York: Bantam Books.

Gratton, L. (2007) *Hot Spots: Why Some Companies Buzz with Energy and Innovation – and Others Don't*, Harlow: Pearson.

Guardian (2014) Asiana airlines crash caused by pilot error and confusion, investigators say, *Guardian*, 24 June. Retrieved from www.theguardian.com/world/2014/jun/24/asiana-crash-san-francsico-controls-investigation-pilot

Guida, R., Trickey, D. and Fregnan, E. (2015) *Managing Challenges Across Cultures: A Multicultural Project Team Toolbox*, Milan: McGraw Hill Education.

Hall, E.T. (1976) *Beyond Culture*, New York: Anchor.

Hammerich, K. and Lewis, R. (2013) *Fish Can't See Water: How National Culture Can Make or Break Your Corporate Strategy*, Chichester: John Wiley.

Hampden-Turner, C. and Trompenaars, F. (2000) *Building Cross-Cultural Competence*, Chichester: John Wiley.

Handy, C. (1993) *Understanding Organizations*, 4th edn, London: Penguin.

Herrero, L. (2008) *Viral Change™: The Alternative to Slow, Painful and Unsuccessful Management of Change in Organisations*, 2nd edn, Meeting Minds.

Hershey, P. and Blanchard, K.H. (1969) *Management of Organizational Behavior: Utilizing Human Resources*, New York: Prentice Hall.

Hinton, P.R. (2020) *Stereotypes and the Construction of the Social World*, Abingdon: Routledge.

Hofstede, G., Hofstede G.J. and Minkov, M. (2010) *Cultures and Organizations: Software of the Mind. Intercultural Cooperation and Its Importance for Survival*, 3rd edn, New York: McGraw Hill.

House, R.J. (ed) (2004) *Culture, Leadership, and Organizations: The GLOBE Study of 62 Societies*, Thousand Oaks, CA: SAGE.

Johansson, F. (2006) *The Medici Effect: What Elephants and Epidemics Can Teach Us About Innovation*, Boston, MA: Harvard Business School Press.

Kahneman, D. (2011) *Thinking, Fast and Slow*, London: Penguin.

Kelly, N. (2021) Implementing inclusive policies across a global organization, *Harvard Business Review*, 2 March. Retrieved from https://hbr.org/2021/03/implementing-inclusive-policies-across-a-global-organization

Kenny, G. (2020) Don't Make the Common M&A Mistake, *Harvard Business Review*, March 16

Kepinski, L. and Nielsen, T.C. (2020) *Inclusion Nudges Guidebook: 100 Practical Examples*, 3rd edn, Independently published.

Kirkman, B., Taras, V. and Steel, P. (2016) Research: the biggest culture gaps are within countries, not between them, *Harvard Business Review*, May 18. Retrieved from https://hbr.org/2016/05/research-the-biggest-culture-gaps-are-within-countries-not-between-them

Kotter, J.P. (1996) *Leading Change*, Boston, MA: Harvard Business School Press.

Kotter, J.P. (2014) *Accelerate: Building Strategic Agility for a Faster-Moving World*, Boston, MA: Harvard Business Review Press.

Kramer, J. (2021) https://humandimensions.com/deep-democracy-the-wisdom-of-the-minority

Kübler-Ross, E. and Kessler, D. (2014) *On Grief and Grieving: Finding the Meaning of Grief through the Five Stages of Loss*, New York: Scribner.

Kurtz, R. (1990) *Body-Centered Psychotherapy: The Hakomi Method*, Mendocino: LifeRythm.

Krogerus, M. and Tschäppeler, R. (2011) *The Decision Book: Fifty Models for Strategic Thinking*, London: Profile Books.

Laurent, A. (1986) The cross-cultural puzzle of international human resource management, *Human Resource Management*, 25(1), 91–102.

References

LeBaron, M. and Pillay, V. (2006) *Conflict across Cultures: A Unique Experience of Bridging Differences*, Boston, MA: Intercultural Press.

Lewis, R.D. (2018) *When Cultures Collide: Leading across Cultures*, 4th edn, London: Nicholas Brealey.

Livermore, D. (2016) Leading a brainstorming session with a cross-cultural team, *Harvard Business Review*, 27 May. Retrieved from https://hbr.org/2016/05/leading-a-brainstorming-session-with-a-cross-cultural-team

Lorde, A. (2007) *Sister Outsider: Essays and Speeches*, Berkeley, CA: Crossing Press.

Luft, J. (1969) *Of Human Interaction*, Palo Alto, CA: National Press Books.

Manian, R. and Naidu, S. (2009) India: a cross-cultural overview of intercultural competence, in D.K. Deardorff (ed.), *The SAGE Handbook of Intercultural Competence*, Thousand Oaks, CA: SAGE, 233–48.

Marx, E. (1999) *Breaking through Culture Shock: What You Need to Succeed in International Business*, London: Nicholas Brealey.

Melaku, T.M., Beeman, A., Smith, D.G. and Johnson W.B. (2020), Be a better ally, *Harvard Business Review*, November–December. Retrieved from https://hbr.org/2016/05/leading-a-brainstorming-session-with-a-cross-cultural-team

Merali, Z. (2005) Exploding the myth of cultural stereotypes, *New Scientist*, 6 October. Retrieved from www.newscientist.com/article/dn8111-exploding-the-myth-of-cultural-stereotypes/

Meyer, E. (2015) *The Culture Map: Decoding How People Think, Lead, and Get Things Done across Cultures*, New York: Public Affairs.

Milne, J. (2018) 'Flip it to test it' – lessons on battling bias from Roche, *Diginomica*, 18 March. Retrieved from https://diginomica.com/flip-it-to-test-it-lessons-on-battling-bias-from-roche

Molinsky, A. (2013) *Global Dexterity. How to Adapt Your Behavior Across Cultures without Losing Yourself in the Process*, Boston, MA: Harvard.

Moosmüller, A. and Schönhuth, M. (2009) Intercultural Competence in German Discourse, in D.K. Deardorff (ed.), *The SAGE Handbook of Intercultural Competence*, Thousand Oaks, CA: SAGE, 225.

Nguyen-Phuong-Mai, M. (2020) *Cross-Cultural Management, with Insights from Brain Science*, New York: Routledge.

Nisbett, R.E. (2003) *The Geography of Thought: How Asians and Westerners Think Differently … and Why* New York: Free Press.

Nwosu, P. (2009) Understanding Africans' conceptualizations of inter-cultural competence, in D.K. Deardorff, *The SAGE Handbook of Intercultural Competence*, Thousand Oaks, CA: SAGE, 158–78.

Oberg, K. (1960) Cultural shock: adjustment to new cultural environ-ments, *Practical Anthropology*, 7, 177–82.

OECD PISA (2018) www.oecd.org/pisa/pisa-2018-global-competence.htm

O'Mara, J., Richter, A., Molefi, N. et al. (2021) *Global Diversity Equity & Inclusion Benchmarks*, Centre for Global Inclusion, https://centre-forglobalinclusion.org/about/

Osland, J. and Bird, A. (2000) Beyond sophisticated stereotyping: Cultural sensemaking in context, *Academy of Management Executive*, 14(1).

Payne, A. and Kaminstein, D. (2021) Effecting real progress in exec-utive diversity and inclusion, *MITSloan Management Review*, 24 February. Retrieved from https://sloanreview.mit.edu/article/effecting-real-progress-in-executive-diversity-and-inclusion/

Pedler, M. (2008) *Action Learning for Managers*, Farnham: Gower.

Pollock, D.C., Van Reken, R.E. and Pollock, V. (2010) *Third Culture Kids: The Experience of Growing Up among Worlds*, 2nd edn, London: Nicholas Brealey.

Progoulaki, M. and Theotokas, I. (2016) Managing culturally diverse maritime human resources as a shipping company's core competency, *Maritime Policy & Management*, 43: 860–73.

Putz, L, E, Schmitz, J. and Walch, K. (2014) *Maximizing Business Results with the Strategic Performance Framework: The Cultural Orientations Guide*, 6th edn, Saline: Training Management Corporation.

Rathje, S. (2009) The definition of culture: An application-oriented over-haul, *Interculture Journal*, 8 September, 35.

Robbins, T. (2021) Code-Switching in the workplace: Being authentic and building resilience, *burrelles.com*, February 23. Retrieved from https://burrelles.com/code-switching-in-the-workplace-being-authen-tic-and-building-resilience/

Rosenberg, M.B. (2015) *Nonviolent Communication: A Language of Compassion*, 3rd edn, Encinitas: Puddle Dancer Press.

Schein, E.H. (2017) *Organizational Culture and Leadership*, 5th edn, Hoboken: John Wiley.

Schulz von Thun, F. (1981) *Miteinander Reden: Störungen und Klärungen*, Hamburg: Rowohlt.

References

Selasi, T. (2014) Don't ask me where I'm from, ask me where I'm local, *TED Global*, October. Retrieved from www.ted.com/talks/taiye_selasi_don_t_ask_where_i_m_from_ask_where_i_m_a_local.

Shaules, J. (2015) *The Intercultural Mind: Connecting Culture, Cognition and Global Living*, Boston, MA: Intercultural Press.

Sigillito Hollema, T. (2020) *Virtual Teams across Cultures: Create Successful Teams around the World*, Twello: Interact Global.

Stepper, J. (2020) *Working Out Loud: A 12-Week Method to Build New Connections, a Better Career, and a More Fulfilling Life*, Vancouver: Page Two.

Taylor, C. (2021) Embracing the Differences, *Change Suite*, Reuters, 8 February. Retrieved from www.reuters.com/article/us-change-suite-neurodiverse-idUSKBN2A80C7

Thaler, R.H. and Sunstein, C.R. (2009) *Nudge: Improving Decisions about Health, Wealth and Happiness*, New York: Penguin Books.

Thomas, A., Kinast, E. (2010) *Handbook of Intercultural Communication and Cooperation, Vol. 1 Basics and Areas of Application*, Göttingen: Vandenhoeck & Ruprecht.

Trompenaars, F. and Prud'homme van Reine, P. (2004) *Managing Change across Corporate Cultures*, Chichester: Capstone Publishing.

Trompenaars, F. and Hampden-Turner, C. (2020), *Riding the Waves of Culture: Understanding Diversity in Global Business*, 4th edn. London: Nicholas Brealey.

Tuckman, B.W. (1965), Developmental Sequence in Small Groups, *Psychological Bulletin*, 63: 384–99.

Tuckman, B.W. and Jensen, M.A.C. (1977) Stages of small-group development revisited, *Group & Organization Studies*, 2(4): 419–27.

University of Bonn (2017) Why expensive wine appears to taste better: It's the price tag: When a bottle costs more, the reward center in the brain plays a trick on us, *ScienceDaily*, August 14. Retrieved from www.sciencedaily.com/releases/2017/08/170814092949.htm

Ury, W. (1991) *Getting Past No: Negotiating in Difficult Situations*, New York: Bantam Books.

Verluyten, S.P. (1999) Conflict avoidance on Thailand, Paper presented at 11th ENCoDe Conference, ESADE, Barcelona, 1–3 July.

Vulpe, T., Kealey, D., Protheroe, D. and MacDonald, D. (2001), *A Profile of the Interculturally Effective Person*, Ottawa: Canadian Foreign Service Institute.

Ward, C., Bochner, S. and Furnham, A. (2001) *The Psychology of Culture Shock*, 2nd edn, Hove: Routledge.

Weinberger, A. (2019) *The Global Mobility Workbook*, 3rd edn, Zurich: Global People Transitions.

Williams, J. (2017) *Don't They Know It's Friday? Cross-Cultural Considerations for Business and Life in the Gulf*, 3rd edn, Motivate Publishing.

Young, P. (2020) Why racial bias is still inherent in biometric tech, *Raconteur*, 28 May. Retrieved from www.raconteur.net/technology/biometrics-ethics-bias/

Index

action learning, 147
active listening, 131–4
adaptation, 22, 155–6
Adler, N., 74, 97
Africa, 6, 31, 46, 62, 69, 149
age, 7, 31–3
agility, 117, 121, 149, 166
algorithms, 49, 57
allyship, 53–4
ambiguity, 2, 21, 69
anti-Semitism, 34
appeal, 78, 81, 128–9
appearance, 51, 64
Arab world, 5, 6, 64–5, 92, 102, 183, 185
artifacts, 12–14
artificial intelligence (AI), 57
Asia, 91
assumptions, 12–14, 99–100, 101
atmosphere, 73, 186, 188
audience, 10, 81–2, 186–7, 189
Australia, 64
Austria, 48, 198

bargaining, 130
Barmeyer, C., 5, 60, 169
beliefs, 11–12, 50, 167–8
bell, ringing, 54
belonging, 27, 35–6
benchmarking, 39–40
bias, 45, 52–4, 62, 140, 179
  affective, 50
  anchoring, 50
  cognitive, 48–51, 58, 75
  confirmation, 50
  groupthink, 50
  halo effect, 50
  horns effect, 50
  similarity, 50
  unconscious, 45–6, 54, 56–7, 183
binational teams, 72, 123–4, 193–5
biodiversity, 28
Black Lives Matter, 40
body distance, 64
body language, 64, 104–5, 132
brain, 43–7, 57–8, 110, 168
  effect of exclusion, 30
brainstorming, 104, 187, 189
Brake, T., 98–9
brand management, 29
Brazil, 116
business travel, 3, 10–11, 152

change curve, 141
change management, 146–7, 149
Charta der Vielfalt (Diversity Charter), 38
checking-in, 81, 185–6
children, 101, 148, 154, 159, 161
China, 6, 32–3, 115
  categorization of objects, 66
  collectivism, 69, 180
  contracts, 130, 185
  counting gestures, 64
  culture, 90, 92, 101, 193–5
  employees, 7, 182

globalization, 3
  identity, 16
  networks, 128–9, 134, 190
  technologies, 100
clothing, 65
code-switching, 166
collectivism, 62, 69, 180, 184, 197
Colombia, 40, 69
communication, 10, 101, 119, 144, 196, 198
  active listening, 131–4
  checking-in, 81, 185–6
  digital, 80, 95–6
  direct and indirect, 67, 106–8, 134, 191, 194
  eye contact, 65, 97, 132, 186
  face-to-face, 2, 80, 101, 108, 173–4, 188
  four sides of message, 78–9
  intercultural, 77–93, 134
  international business English, 85–7
  low-context, 190
  non-verbal, 64–5
  phatic, 89
  problematic, 145
  processes, 118
  turn-taking, 65, 103, 190–1
  virtual, 97, 98, 104–5, 190
conflict, 130–1, 133–4
  avoiding, 131
  eye contact, 65
  resolution, 117, 134–6, 197
context, 60–1, 79, 170
  high, 66, 92, 134, 191, 196
  low, 66, 118, 190
corporate communications, 10
country profiles, 175
COVID-19, 29, 35, 95
critical incidents, 62, 71–4, 173–4
  be prepared, 83, 187–8
  the budget meeting, 83, 188
  checking-in, 81, 185–6
  congratulations, 72, 184
  how many parts? 72, 184
  leadership training, 83–4, 188
  missing the flight, 71, 183
  phones in meetings, 72, 184
  the retreat, 73, 185
  silence is golden, 102, 190–1
  slot reservation, 73–4, 185
  the window, 136, 197
criticism, 79, 105
cross-border business, 4
cultural adjustment, 152–5, 157
cultural bridging, 169–71
cultural dimensions, 61–3, 75–6
cultural due diligence, 143
cultural filters, 49–50, 52
cultural intelligence, 20, 99
cultural noise, 80, 167
cultural transitions, 157–9
culture
  corporate, 13–14
  department, 14
  function, 5–6, 15
  fuzzy, 11
  length of service, 15

location, 73
models, 62–3
position, 14–15
professional, 14
sector, 13
site, 14
team, 14
Culture Navigation System, 63, 71, 170
culture shock, 152–6
curiosity, 164
customers, 5, 6, 29, 73–4, 129

decision-making, 58, 117–18, 125, 143, 186, 194
Deep Democracy, 149
DEIB (diversity, equity, inclusion and belonging), 27, 35–7, 39, 40
design, 146
development, 24, 40, 55–6
team, 120–1
differences, 2–6, 22–3, 27–41, 61, 171 (see also diversity; Wheel of Difference)
celebrating, 169
and leadership, 111–14
between neighbouring countries, 144–5
in power distance, 115–17, 185
dilemma reconciliation, 145
discrimination, 37, 40, 45, 56
age, 31
legislation, 28
neurodiversity, 34
racial, 46, 51
dispersed teams, 4, 96, 97
DiStefano, L., 22, 169
diverse teams, 4, 104, 159
diversity, 27–41 (see also differences)
celebrating, 169
cognitive, 34–5
complexity of, 163–4
impact of, 1–16, 139
and leadership, 124–5
and recruitment, 55
training programmes, 56
diversity audit, 39–40
diversity dimensions, 29, 30–5, 39, 52
diversity initiatives, 27, 40–1

education, 49, 104, 115, 172, 194
emails, 77–8, 80, 101, 119
emotional intelligence (EQ), 20
emotions, 30, 47–8, 50, 108, 131, 140
empathy, 9, 165–6
engineering, 5, 8, 161
STEM subjects, 29
environment, health and safety (EHS), 9
equality, 35
equity, 27, 35–6, 54
ethnicity, 31, 33
Europe, 172, 182, 183, 185–6
body distance, 64
stereotypes, 48–9
tomography scanners, 6
Walmart in, 5
exclusion, 30, 36–7
extroverts, 104
eye contact, 65, 97, 132, 186

face, saving, 90, 133, 134, 137, 196
face-to-face meetings, 2, 80, 101, 108, 173–4, 188
facial expressions, 65, 79
facial recognition, 46
family status, 31

feedback, 104–5, 117, 194, 195
blurring, 107–8
burger technique, 106–7
lack of, 147
WWW, 106
femininity, 62
finance, 7
Fisher, R., 137
France, 116–17, 119
functions, 5–6, 15

Gabon, 11
gender, 33, 39, 53
gender identity, 33
generation, 31–3, 97
Germany, 38, 193–5
checking-in, 186
clothing, 181
criticism, 105
humour, 188
management styles, 119, 191, 198
power distance, 116, 185
preparation, 187–8
presentations, 81
qualifications, 115
race, 34
restaurant and bar bills, 92
task orientation, 183
uncertainty avoidance, 184
weekends, 102
gestures, 64, 79, 104–5
Ghana, 51
gifts, 90
global competence, 20
global workplace, 104, 153
globalization, 2–3, 5–6, 9, 95
GLOBE (Global Leadership and Organizational Behavior Effectiveness), 62
glocalization, 145–6
goals, 99, 135–6, 171
Greek language, 48, 188
guanxi, 128–9

Hall, E., 66
Hindu culture, 64
Hofstede, G., 69, 75, 115–18, 165, 173
hot spots, 147–8
human resources (HR), 7, 141–2, 143, 153, 197–8
humour, 86, 108, 182, 186, 188

iceberg model, 11, 152
identity, 15–16
cultural, 74
gender, 33
group, 12–13
racial, 33–4
tribal, 31
virtual, 108
Implicit Association Test (IAT), 52
inclusion, 37, 40
diversity, equity, inclusion and belonging (DEIB), 35–6
language of, 53
in leadership, 111–25
organizations, 37–9, 43, 99
vs. unconscious bias, 45–6, 52
India, 6, 63, 108, 115–16
individualism, 62, 69, 106, 184
indulgence, 62
influencing, 7, 13–14, 127–37
cultural, 6, 46, 179
groupthink, 50

Index

by peers, 148
pull technique, 128
push technique, 128
unconscious bias, 55, 57
without authority, 193
information technology (IT), 10
innovation, 29, 96, 147–9
integration, 37, 51, 144 (*see also* collectivism)
mapping, bridging, integrating (MBI) model, 169
interaction, 56, 67, 167, 173–4, 189
audience, 186
intercultural assessment, 23–5, 160
intercultural cocktail, 59–76
intercultural communication, 77–93, 134
intercultural competence, 2, 17–25, 62–3, 180–1
intercultural management, 146
intercultural teams, 122
effectiveness, 97–8, 110
intercultural toolkit, 128
interculturalism, 47, 153
domestic, 161
individual, 15
support, 159–60
international assignment, 4, 151–62
international business English, 85–7
international teams, 4, 8, 72, 96–7, 122–4, 191, 194
interpreters, 87–8, 164
introverts, 102–3, 189
Islamic culture, 46, 64, 102
Italy, 50

Japan, 66, 92–3, 115–16, 166, 184, 191
job applications, 7, 38, 46, 50, 195
Johari House, 168
just-in-time (JIT), 149

Kahneman, D., 48
kaizen, 149
Korea, 5, 50, 92
Kotter, J., 140

languages, 69, 87, 158–9, 182
Latin America, 6, 40, 64, 91
leadership, 70, 83–4, 188
cooperative, 122
delegative, 122
directive, 122
inclusive, 111–24
situational, 121–4
supportive, 122
leadership styles, 115, 128
leadership training, 83–4, 115, 188
learning, 22, 147, 158, 171–2, 175
learning diary, 176
LGBT+ community, 28, 33, 40, 46
locality, 65, 97, 143, 155, 158, 164
glocalization, 145–6
long term orientation, 62
loyalty, 69, 123, 194

M&A (mergers and acquisitions), 139, 142–5
management, 14–15, 198
cultural differences, 115, 119, 182, 185
gender, 39
vs. leadership, 111
team assistants, 10
managing events, 70
mapping, bridging, integrating (MBI) model, 169
marginalization, 53–4, 97
marketing, 6, 76
masculinity, 62, 117

mediation, 121–2
medical services, 10–11
meetings, 82–7, 101, 103
in China, 190, 194
face-to-face, 2, 80, 101, 108, 173–4, 188
in Germany, 195
language of, 155
phones in, 72, 167, 184
virtual, 54, 100–1, 103, 109, 112, 190–1
melting pot, 37
mental ability, 31, 34–5
mental shortcuts, 47
mentorship, 56
mergers and acquisitions (M&A), 139, 142–5
microaggressions, 51
mindfulness, 169
monocultural teams, 29, 96, 97, 99–100, 179
motivation, 45, 99, 119
multicollectivity, 15, 167
Muslims *see* Islamic culture

national cultures, 15, 59, 62, 75, 173, 198
nationality, 34
negotiating, 8, 87, 129–31, 132–3, 196
neurodiversity, 34–5
neuroscience, 30, 43–7, 57–8, 110, 168
Nigeria, 51
nomads, 3, 4
nudging, 54–5

OAR approach, ix, 176
observations, 176
onion model, 12, 13–14
Organisation for Economic Co-operation and
Development, 20
organizational dimensions, 24, 31
organizations, 37–41, 139–45, 148, 162
change, 54–7
Germany, 198
global, 105, 127–8, 145
in other countries, 116

pain, 11, 30
peach and coconut, 67–8
perception, 43–4
person orientation, 183
phatic communication, 89
physical ability, 29
physical contact, 64
planning, 184–6, 190
political views, 31
polyculturalism, 167
posture, 64, 132
power distance, 69–70, 115–17
praise, 105, 107, 184
prejudice, 45
presentations, 81–2, 189
procedures, 118
processes, 118
recruitment and development, 55–6
procurement, 8
production, 8
project management, 114, 191, 193
public and private spheres, 67–8, 88

qualifications, 115, 130, 174

race, 31, 33–4
racism, 29, 34, 40–1
recruitment, 40, 55
re-entry, 156, 158, 162

regional identity, 3, 31, 143
regional offices, 14, 40, 97, 127–8, 163
relationships, 108–9, 128–9, 148
  business, 21, 24, 87–8
  context, 66
  personal, 54, 159, 196
religion, 8, 31, 34, 91, 101–2 (*see also* Islamic culture)
research, 12
  communication, 107, 119
  cultural dimensions, 61–3, 75–6
  on discrimination, 46
  on diversity, 28
  on hierarchies, 115–16
  on intercultural teams, 97–8
  neuroscientific, 110, 168
  on social exclusion, 30
  on stereotypes, 49
  wine-tasting, 44–5
responsibility, 57, 99, 122–4, 193
  corporate, 40
restraint, 62
role models, 56
rules, 70, 118, 128
  attitudes to, 9, 185
  clothing, 65
  on gifts, 90
  health and safety, 9
Russia, 6, 65, 115, 172

salad bowl, 37
sales, 73–4, 81, 84, 91, 127–9, 132–3
sales channels, 143
Saudi Arabia, 6, 163
Schein, E., 12
Schulz von Thun, F., 78
self-disclosure, 78–9
sexual orientation, 29, 31, 33
shipping, 9
silence, 65, 102–3, 190–1
situation, 176
situational leadership, 121–4
small talk, 88–90, 165, 183
smell, 65
social media, 49, 53, 161, 171
socializing, 49, 67–8, 88, 92–3
socio-economic status, 31
software architecture, 8–9
space, 67–8, 96, 172
spouses, 4, 156, 158–9, 161
STEM subjects, 29
stereotypes, 14, 48–50, 74–5, 165, 186
strategy, 143, 146
structures, 116–17, 193
Sweden, 5, 116, 190–1
synergies, 145–6, 169, 171

team assistants, 10, 164
team development, 120–1
teams, 14
  binational, 72, 123–4, 193–5
  dispersed, 4, 96, 97
  diverse, 4, 104, 159
  intercultural, 97–8, 110, 122
  international, 4, 8, 72, 96–7, 122–4, 191, 194
  monocultural, 29, 96, 97, 99–100, 179
  virtual, 95–110, 120
tendencies, 74–6
third culture kids (TCKs), 159
three-factor model, 60, 169

time
  event-related, 70
  monochronic, 70, 184, 186, 190
  past–present–future, 71, 129
  polychronic, 70, 184, 186–7
time zones, 96, 97, 101, 191
touch, 64
training, 23–4, 38, 56, 171–7
  anti-discrimination, 52
  anti-racism, 41
  for international assignments, 161–2
  leadership, 83–4, 115, 188
transformation, 172
transitions, 157–9
tree model, 11
Trompenaars, F., 62, 70, 145, 173
Tuckman, B., 120–1
turn-taking, 65, 103, 190–1

UAE (United Arab Emirates), 102
ubuntu, 69
UK (United Kingdom)
  diversity, 28
  gestures, 64
  indirect communication, 67
  inductive style, 81
  management, 117, 119, 191
  motivation, 119
  phatic communication, 89
  planning and flexibility, 184
  power distance, 116
  punctuality, 91
  qualifications, 115
  restaurant and bar bills, 92
  socializing, 88, 92–3
  turn-taking, 190–1
uncertainty avoidance, 62, 69, 118–19, 184, 186, 190, 196
USA
  categorization of objects, 66
  checking-in, 186
  feedback styles, 105
  inductive style, 81
  management, 115, 119
  motivation, 119
  multiculturalism, 37, 61
  person orientation, 183
  phatic communication, 89
  power distance, 116
  preparation, 187–8
  procedures, 118
  race, 33, 40–1
  recruitment, 7, 55
  socializing, 91, 92
  Walmart in, 5

values, 11–12, 14, 40, 62, 75, 128, 167–8
viral change™, 148
virtual collaboration, 95–110
virtual meetings, 54, 100–1, 103, 109, 112, 190–1
virtual teams, 95–110, 120
vision, 14, 40, 111, 140–1, 143
VUCA (volatility, uncertainty, complexity, ambiguity), 2, 28, 177

Wheel of Difference, 30–2, 170, 173
working hours, 102
working out loud, 148
World Values Survey (WVS), 61–2

About the author

Robert Gibson is an interculturalist with over 30 years' experience of intercultural competence development in business and education.

He was responsible for intercultural consultancy and training in the global engineering corporation Siemens AG for 18 years. As well as leading a team of intercultural experts, he managed international change projects on topics as diverse as Post-Merger Integration, Performance Management, Customer Understanding and Leadership Culture. He was a member of the Global Expert Team which designed and implemented an award-winning Diversity and Inclusion initiative for over 230,000 employees worldwide.

He was first involved in international education while a school teacher in rural England during which time he ran projects in Germany, Poland and Hungary for the Council of Europe and UNESCO. He went on to become a lecturer at the University of Munich, an adviser on vocational education to the Bavarian Ministry of Education, and Head of Department at Ingolstadt School of Management. He has been a guest lecturer at the University of the Arts in Berlin and an adjunct professor at the Business School of the University of Bologna, teaching Intercultural Management on Global MBA and MA programmes.

His publications include *Intercultural Business Communication* (Oxford University Press, 2002) and over 70 articles on intercultural communication for the magazine *Business Spotlight*. He is a former vice-president of the Society for Intercultural Education,

Training and Research (SIETAR Europa) and a founder and member of the Advisory Board of SIETAR Deutschland.

He grew up in London and studied at the Universities of Oxford and Exeter in the UK before moving to Germany in 1985. He is currently based in Munich and works as a freelance consultant, facilitator and trainer.

Acknowledgements

My thanks go to all those interculturalists who have so generously shared their ideas with me over the years. Since attending its congress in Kilkenny in Ireland in 1990, I have benefited enormously from being involved in the Society for Intercultural, Education, Training and Research (SIETAR), the leading interdisciplinary, global network of intercultural professionals.

My colleagues and clients at Siemens AG provided me with invaluable insights into business from within a global corporation. I am especially grateful to Tim Bookas for opening the door, as well as Zailiang Tang and Theresia Tauber for their inspiration and support during my 18 years in the company.

I feel privileged to have had the opportunity to teach at the University of Bologna Business School in the magnificent setting of the Villa Guastavillani. Its international students have stimulated me to think more deeply about working with different professional cultures around the world from food and wine in Italy to green energy in Nigeria. Thanks to Gabriele Morandin and Marcello Russo.

Ian McMaster encouraged me to reflect on my experiences and develop my ideas by providing me with a regular column in *Business Spotlight* magazine. Thanks to him and Sonia Brough for helping me prepare the manuscript for publication, Hennes Elbert for the graphics and Holly Bennion at Nicholas Brealey, who quickly recognized the potential of the book.

Last but by no means least, I would like to thank my wife, Emily, for providing me with the chance to experience China from the inside and, above all, for her unconditional love and support.

Would you like your people to read this book?

If you would like to discuss how you could bring these ideas to your team, we would love to hear from you. Our titles are available at competitive discounts when purchased in bulk across both physical and digital formats. We can offer bespoke editions featuring corporate logos, customized covers, or letters from company directors in the front matter can also be created in line with your special requirements.

We work closely with leading experts and organizations to bring forward-thinking ideas to a global audience. Our books are designed to help you be more successful in work and life.

For further information, or to request a catalogue, please contact: **business@johnmurrays.co.uk**
sales-US@nicholasbrealey.com (North America only)

Nicholas Brealey Publishing is an imprint of John Murray Press.